W9-CBC-436

Acknowledgments

Grace Hughes-Manor made invaluable research contributions to my work on this book; without her help and advice, it would never have come into existence. My editor Jim Ellison showed patience, good humor, and a true baseball fan's perspective as the project took shape. Andrew Cote offered early support and library help. Bob Tragert helped with more research later on in the project and provided general moral support. Glenn KnicKrehm offered his customarily unfailing encouragement and generosity as this book moved forward; much of this book was written at his home, for which many thanks are due. Leslie Hamilton helped me to clear the decks and focus on the project in the first place. The staff of the Peabody Institute Library in Danvers, Massachusetts, was most helpful. David, Julia, and Stephen Toropov brought their special brand of enthusiasm to the project. My wife Mary was patient, resourceful, and a source of endless good humor.

······································ ◯ ······································

Truth is always exciting. Speak it, then. Life is dull without it.
—PEARL S. BUCK

I really didn't say everything I said.
—YOGI BERRA

You could look it up.
—CASEY STENGEL

Babe Ruth "called his shot" in the 1932 World Series...
didn't he?

Dizzy Dean won 30 games during the 1934 season...
didn't he?

Jackie Robinson was the first black baseball player in
major-league history...wasn't he?

The New York Mets were the worst team in baseball
history...weren't they?

The surprising answer to all these questions is no—as you
will learn when you read *50 Biggest Baseball Myths* by
Brandon Toropov.

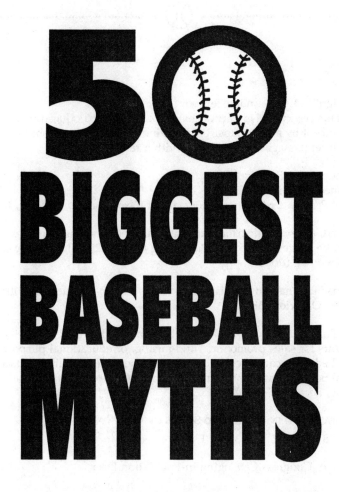

50 BIGGEST BASEBALL MYTHS

BRANDON TOROPOV

A Citadel Press Book
Published by Carol Publishing Group

Copyright © 1997 Brandon Toropov
All rights reserved. No part of this book may be reproduced in any
form, except by a newspaper or magazine reviewer who wishes to
quote brief passages in connection with a review.

A Citadel Press Book
Published by Carol Publishing Group
Citadel Press is a registered trademark of Carol Communications, Inc.

Editorial, sales and distribution, rights and permissions inquiries
should be addressed to Carol Publishing Group, 120 Enterprise Avenue,
Secaucus, N.J. 07094

In Canada: Canadian Manda Group, One Atlantic Avenue, Suite 105,
Toronto, Ontario M6K 3E7

Carol Publishing Group books may be purchased in bulk at special
discounts for sales promotion, fund-raising, or educational purposes.
Special editions can be created to specifications. For details, contact
Special Sales Department, Carol Publishing Group, 120 Enterprise
Avenue, Secaucus, N.J. 07094.

MANUFACTURED IN THE UNITED STATES OF AMERICA
10 9 8 7 6 5 4 3 2 1

Library of Congress Cataloging-in-Publication Data

Toropov, Brandon.
    50 biggest baseball myths / Brandon Toropov.
        p. cm.
    "A Citadel Press book."
    Includes bibliographical references (p.   ).
    ISBN 0–8065–1875–8 (pb)
    1. Baseball—United States—Miscellanea.   2. Baseball—United
States—History.   I. Title.
    GV863.A1T65   1997
    796.357'0973—dc21   97–2193
                                                           CIP

To those who can peacefully resolve thorny baseball conflicts, such as the unpardonable strike of 1994, and ensure that such dire lapses never take place again.

Introduction

As I was wrapping up this book, a friend of mine called. I could tell from the moment I heard his voice over the phone that he had a troubled heart. "I heard about that book you're writing," he said. "Is it really true that you're debunking the called shot?"

He was referring to the famous incident (or, as I prefer to think of it, nonincident) in the 1932 World Series, in which Babe Ruth supposedly predicted his home run against Chicago pitcher Charlie Root. I informed my friend that, yes, Ruth seemed to be on the record as having denied that the "called shot" took place, and that that pretty much settled the matter as far as I was concerned.

The feeling of quiet betrayal on the other end of the line was palpable. It was as though I had backed a truck into my friend's family room or taken away a family heirloom of long standing. In a way, I imagine, I had.

The question occurred to me: Is this book an exercise in sadism? Will it dishearten more fans than it fascinates?

Will *50 Biggest Baseball Myths* stand as another monument to cynicism in an already cynical world? Is it only going to deprive people of their dreams, of their favorite stories, of their idealistic notions about the game they love?

It certainly isn't intended that way. To me, baseball history is a magnificent, swirling pageant that gets *more* fascinating as it gets more accurate. When you "bag" a cherished baseball story—that is to say, when you learn, at long last, the actual facts behind a long-repeated tale, or discover the truth behind a popular misconception—it seems to me that you have the opportunity to acquire a greater, not lesser, respect for the game. That's what happened during that conversation with my friend. We spent a long time talking about the "called shot" phenomenon, about the sports media in the thirties, about the sports media today. At the end of my call with him, I felt as though he'd come away a little less innocent about the supposedly superhuman abilities of Babe Ruth...and a little more curious about the reliable human tendency to ascribe superhuman tendencies to popular figures in general, and baseball players in particular. This seemed a laudable enough outcome, and a vindication of sorts that this book might *not* bring a more jaded attitude to an already jaded sports world.

Still, I realize there are those who will argue against this book's purpose, along these or similar lines: "Baseball is, to a larger degree than most sports, a game of myth, of story, of fable, of heroes we delight in transforming into figures who are bigger than life. In baseball, we seem to *want* exaggerations and miracles and extraordinary feats. We live for events like Mazeroski's Series-winning home run in the final game of the 1960 World Series, or Joe Carter's Series-winning home run in the final game of the 1993 World Series, or Ruth's "called shot" in the 1932 World Series. We gain a sense of purpose and meaning and resolution from talking about these moments, because we want more from baseball than we want from other sports. We want *redemption*. So why go out of your way to shatter all the icons? Why dig around in the library in search of misconceptions surrounding the National Pastime? Maybe your "misconception" is my "defining moment." Why try to take that moment away?

Why shatter the myth? Because Mazeroski and Carter *did* do something (comparatively) miraculous in 1960 and 1993, respectively, and Ruth, for all his other mammoth accomplishments, really *didn't* in 1932. In 1960, Mazeroski's blow broke an ninth-inning tie, marked the first time a World Series ended with a home run, and put the final exclamation point on one of the greatest upsets in baseball history. In 1993, Joe Carter's blast in Game Six went Mazeroski one better by taking a team that was *behind in the score* and turning it into a World Series championship squad with a single swing of the bat. Those are truly remarkable accomplishments, and they've been duly celebrated and discussed since they happened. But they haven't been celebrated and discussed at anything like the level the Babe's nonexistent "called shot" has. What did Ruth do in that game? He hit a fifth-inning home run, his second of the game, that put his team ahead in Game Three of a Series that his team eventually swept. That's great, but it's simply not in the same league as the accomplishments of the other two men. To my way of thinking, Mazeroski and Carter get shortchanged unless you look at all three events as they ought to be examined. (That is, in full possession of the facts.) Placing an imaginary accomplishment above the real thing—as people have done with the "called shot" story and any number of others—only distorts and minimizes the real "defining moments" in baseball, of which there are plenty.

Why shatter the myth? Because the truth is often far more interesting than the fiction. One of the most impossible-sounding—and hence frequently dismissed—stories about Negro Leagues great Cool Papa Bell turns out to be based in fact. For my part, I think it's worth a little digging, a little time, to track down the details when they bring the whole picture into clearer focus... because there is the very real incentive that, every once in a while, you may just come across a *better* story that has the added advantage of being, well, true. (See Myth 9.)

Why shatter the myth? Because the nature of the fiction often tells us a lot about who we were at the time. In 1945, a war-weary America may have *wanted* to believe that there had never been a player who'd overcome handicaps in the way that one-armed outfielder Pete Gray of the St. Louis Browns did. There were several. Similarly, Depression-era baseball fans, in quest of heroes shortly before the election of Franklin Roosevelt, probably needed Babe Ruth to have called his shot in the 1932 World Series.

Why shatter the myth? Because, frankly, it's a lot of fun to get to the bottom of things. Lots of people say the 1962 New York Mets were the worst team of all time, but there's a twinge of triumph that accompanies learning that they weren't. It's like finding out that you've been given a map that's incorrectly marked, and then unhesitatingly pulling out a marker and putting a line where the right turn needs to be.

Much of what follows is likely to be assigned to the "we'll never really know" category—or denied outright—by those who have difficulty, for whatever reason, parting company with an idea, story, or report that has held currency for a long time. That's the status a good many people assign to the famous story of Babe Ruth's ability to predict his home-run shot in the World Series of 1932. Obviously, I disagree, and I think with good reason. I realize that a lot of what appears in this book is worth arguing about. That's half the fun of being a baseball fan. There will probably always be people who insist that Dizzy Dean won 30 games in 1934, or that Ty Cobb hit a total of 4,191 base hits over the course of his glorious career. But things didn't look that way to me, and for my part, I don't think they'll look that way to you after you've finished the entries in question. It's your call.

All I've done in this book is make an accounting of the facts I was able to ascertain, facts that led me to believe that the established, perceived way of looking at certain trends and incidents in baseball was probably faulty. I've made the clearest cases I can for the entries that follow, and I have tried to follow the most responsible path possible in making those cases. It's certainly your right as a fan to disagree—but read the entry first!

And let's be clear about one thing: The act of arguing about the minutiae of baseball history is, in and of itself, an important part of the National Pastime, and it may be one of the most enjoyable parts. How else are we going to make it through the winter to spring training if we don't have some story that can be counted on to inspire a little good-natured baseball discord with our friends? I certainly don't intend to curtail that activity forever by passing along the accounts that follow, and I don't for a moment pretend that there aren't people out there who know more about many of these incidents than I was able to track down.

If you feel you've come across solid evidence that points in another direction than the one I've followed, by all means let me know. I realize that baseball is a game with a rich history whose events sometimes look different to different people. What's more, new research is constantly turning up more and more authoritative information about the game's great, and not-so-great, figures (although this new information doesn't always lead to widespread reassessment of the most commonly circulated stories). In this book, I've done my level best to get to the bottom of what appeared to me to be the most important unfounded notions connected with the National Pastime. If you think I've missed a step on one or more of the entries, or if you know of a story that *should* have been debunked within these covers, but wasn't, please write me, care of the publisher. I'll be eager to hear what you have to say.

So—let's get started. What does it all look like? How does it work? What can you expect to find here, and how is the material arranged?

By means of an admittedly subjective ascending ranking, from number 50 to number 1, the *50 Biggest Baseball Myths* details the biggest misconceptions, exaggerations, and flat-out lies in the history of baseball—as this baseball fan saw them. I hope the book turns out to be as much fun for you to read as it was for me to write.

And that's no lie.

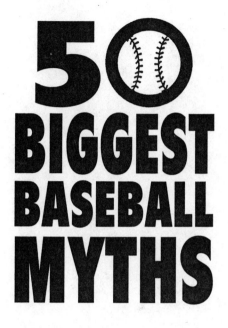

MYTH 50

The 1962 New York Mets Were the Worst Team in the History of Major-League Baseball

The record in question's surprising at first;
Casey's boys weren't even second to worst!

Pennant contenders? Maybe not. But the 1962 New York Mets of Marvelous Marv Throneberry and Choo Choo Coleman fame, piloted by Casey Stengel, would have had to have done a good deal worse than they did to win the coveted (?) title of "worst big-league team ever." You think 40–120 is a lousy enough record to take the "crown"? Think again.

Consider the hapless 1899 Cleveland Spiders. The team finished a seemingly impossible 84 games behind the front-running Brooklyn outfit in the National League that year; New York's sixty-and-a-half game finish behind the pennant-winning San Francisco Giants in 1962 looks positively robust by comparison.

The Spiders won 20 games and lost 134, for an anemic winning percentage of .130. Cleveland finished dead last in both the team batting average and team earned-run average categories. Their pitching staff boasted, in "Cold Water" Jim Hughey, a 30-game *loser*. Hughey's bloated 5.41 earned-run average was the best among the team's starters, but his status as "ace," such as it was, didn't keep him from getting shellacked on a regular basis throughout his career. The thirty-year-old right-hander had posted an abysmal 7–24 record with the Cardinals the year before; he led the National League in losses during the doomed 1899 Cleveland campaign, finishing up with 30 losses and only 4 victories. His nickname resulted, not from his ability to douse the prospects of victory, as one might imagine, but from his hometown in Michigan, Coldwater. In the annals of single-season starting pitching futility, Hughey certainly deserves notice for his meager .118 winning percentage in 34 decisions during 1899. Cold Water Jim was out of baseball by the end of the 1900 season; he closed out his career with a less than distinguised 29–80 record. His only winning season had been his first, in which he'd gone 1–0.

Then there's the 1889 Louisville Colonels, who posted a scary 27–111 record in the American Assocation. They burned their way through four managers. (The one who lasted longest was the intriguingly named "Chicken" Wolf, who skippered for 66 games, less than half the season.) The Colonels posted the worst team batting average in the league. Their pitching staff included a 29-game loser, (Red Ehret, who went 10–29) and a 30-game loser (John Ewing, who was 6–30). They only played 138 games, but still managed to finish sixty-six and a half games behind first-place Brooklyn!

Now suppose you want to argue that the Spiders' and Colonels' futility shouldn't count, because they played in the nineteenth century. On this point I would disagree, and strongly, but even conceding the point for the sake of argument, I note that the Mets must still contend with two teams: the 1916 Philadelphia Athletics, whose season was a truly frightening one for all concerned, and the 1935 Boston

Braves, who had a year so bad they tried—and failed—to change their name in subsequent seasons.

The A's won 36 games and lost 117 in 1917, for a winning percentage of .235. This easily outdistances the Mets, who managed to win a healthy one-quarter of their games. Jack Nabors posted a 1–20 record for the A's that year; Tom Sheehan was nipping at his heels with a 1–16 mark. The team had a hunchbacked batboy they kept around for good luck. He died during the season.

And to think that Connie Mack's team had cruised to a pennant just two years earlier! Surely this must stand in greater (lesser?) regard than the Mets' antiseason, if only on principle, because everyone *knew* the Mets had the limited potential of an expansion team. (To be fair, however, many of the standouts from the 1914 season were no longer on board.)

The 1935 Braves, inexplicably overlooked by many who make reference to baseball's all-time worst-team list, won only 38 games and lost 115, for a winning percentage of .248. That mark also underwhelms the Mets' 1962 percentage. Predictably Boston had the league's worst earned-run average, lowest batting average, and saddest starting pitching statistics. (Ben Cantwell went 4–25.) Surprisingly the team also boasted the league's top home-run and RBI man in center fielder Wally Berger. But that was the team's only real bright spot. The Braves were so bad in 1935 that they rechristened themselves the Bees in the following season, hoping to make a clean break with the past. They still finished in the second division—although not in the cellar—and after a few years they reverted to the older name Braves. (For an explanation of this name's often-misunderstood origin, see Myth 17.)

The 1962 Mets did indeed find any number of inventive ways to lose, as their many chroniclers have claimed, but history is a cruel mistress, and Stengel's boys must take their lumps: They weren't the worst ever. Even in losing, they are denied the superlatives. Which counts for something, I guess.

In summary: Even the *name* "Cleveland Spiders" has the Mets beaten hands down. Give the Marvel No-Prize to the boys of the summer of 1899.

MYTH 49

Dave Winfield Threw a Baseball That Killed a Sea Gull in Midflight

The death of the bird was the talk of the town,
But whoever said Dave brought the poor thing down?

The incident under discussion took place on August 4, 1983. It generated a minor media spasm at the time, but in the years since has typically been recounted in a single sentence. This has led to much misunderstanding among the baseball fans who have heard it and passed it along to their friends. What people usually hear is something like this: *Between innings of a game against the Blue Jays in Toronto, Yankee outfielder Dave Winfield threw a warmup toss at a seagull, killing the bird.*

This summary is not, strictly speaking, *incorrect*, but it does leave one with a mental picture that is not completely in accordance with the facts. The image—that of Winfield hauling off a throw and striking a bird in midair—has left any number of fans wondering about Winfield's humane instincts and amazed at his ability to hit a moving target. According to Dom Forker's *Ultimate Baseball Quiz Book*, Winfield tossed his warm-up throw *after the seagull had been resting on the grass.* Evidently the ball struck the (already wounded) bird, and it died.

A question arises. If a bird flew into *your* place of

employment, would *you* try to get rid of it, or see to it that someone else did?

Toronto police arrested the Yankee outfielder; he was later charged with cruelty to animals, but the charges were eventually dropped.

To this day, however, a good many baseball fans believe that Winfield employed pinpoint throwing accuracy to down a passing gull. That would have been quite a feat—and one worthy of Winfield's early reputation as a star pitcher in college. (He posted a 13–1 record for the University of Minnesota Gophers.) But it's not what happened.

For what it's worth, the Braves' Dion James hit a flying bird with a *batted* ball during a 1987 game against the New York Mets at Shea Stadium. The bird, a dove, fell to the ground and died (much to the confusion of the Mets); James was awarded a ground-rule double.

In summary: Winfield's extraordinary career is memorable for his superb on-the-field contributions—witness his multiple All-Star years and Gold Glove awards, his league-leading RBI total in 1979, and his five straight hundred-RBI seasons between 1982 and 1986—and for his ability to outnegotiate, weather the wrath of, and generally be far, far less of a jerk than George Steinbrenner. (Come to think of it, that last item isn't really that much of an accomplishment, but Winfield still deserves credit for acquitting himself well during one of the most sordid Steinbrenner Fits, the Howie Spira mess.) His involvement in the infamous, and, often, inaccurately told seagull incident, by contrast, is not worth a tenth of the attention it has aroused.

MYTH 48

Candy Cummings Invented the Curveball

The curve is the pitch that transformed the game—
Did Candy invent it? And earn his claim to fame?

Did Candy Cummings invent the curveball? The answer appears to be no.

File this one under "Creation Myths, Secondary." What we're looking at is a chain of reasoning that runs something like this:

- Curveballs don't just happen. For ordinary mortals, they're tough to learn to throw.
- Curveballs confuse batters. The appearance of the curveball was a landmark development in the history of the game.
- *Someone* must have invented the thing, and that someone deserves to be in the Hall of Fame.

It all seems plausible enough on the surface, but that third point is where things begin to get a little boggy. Much of the game's early history is devilishly hard to trace, and this is an instance of just such difficulty. There may be a plaque in Cooperstown bearing Candy Cummings's name, and it may credit him with the development of the curve, but he appears to have had less to do with the development of that pitch than with that of any number of others.

Cummings is said to have gotten the idea for the curve while throwing a clamshell, and to have tried doggedly to duplicate the shell's path with a baseball. He claimed that he first pitched the curve in 1864, and introduced it to organized baseball in 1867, while pitching for a Brooklyn team. He even claimed to have amazed some physics students during an exhibition of his newfangled pitch.

All of this sounds impressive. None of it is documented.

The first authenticated report of a curveball appears in 1870, when someone set up a test for pitcher Fred Goldsmith. Two longish stakes were placed in a straight line between the mound and home plate. Goldsmith took his place on the mound, reared back, and threw. The ball glided past the stakes.

Baseball legend has it that Goldsmith, who was evidently crushed at the baseball establishment's failure to recognize him as the developer of the curveball, died holding a yellowed clipping recounting the 1870 demonstration. He passed on in 1939, the same year Cummings made it to the Hall of Fame.

Was Goldsmith's 1870 pitch the *first* curveball ever thrown? No. Any number of players had claimed the pitch by this point. It had been a lively topic of discussion for some time, and was thought by many to be an optical illusion. Hence the get-to-the-facts-of-the-matter approach people took in evaluating Goldsmith's delivery.

Way back in 1859, a second baseman for an Amherst team claimed that his pitcher, Henry O. Hyde, "had a wonderful knack of making the ball curve in to the catcher." Such observations were common around this time.

The whole picture is a murky one, but it's a picture that seems to exclude the diminutive Cummings, who claimed that he developed the pitch to compensate for his 120-pound, five-foot-nine-inch frame. Despite a 1908 article he wrote claiming credit for "the first curve," and the willingness of the baseball establishment to line up dutifully behind his claim, Cummings's account is dubious. Many people claimed to have been the first to throw the curveball. Cummings was one of them. (An interesting side note: Cummings *was* the first big-league pitcher to pitch two complete games in a single day, a feat he pulled off in 1876.)

Cummings seems to have been one of the earliest players to deliver the curve reliably—he went 16–8 for Hartford in 1876—but he has no overriding claim to being the pitch's inventor. Who does? Who knows?

Cummings did, however, serve as the president of the International Association, baseball's first minor league. He also invented a coupling device for railroad cars!

Among many who deplored the "deceptive" but steadily more popular innovation known as the curveball were the president of Harvard and the legendary American poet Walt Whitman. The university president expressed dismay that his own school's team would stoop to such underhanded tactics to win games. When a friend visited Whitman in 1889 and started talking baseball, the poet asked, "In baseball, is it the rule that the fellow pitching the ball aims to pitch it in such a way the batter cannot hit it? Gives it a what-not—so it slides off, or won't be struck fairly?" Told that this was in fact the case, Whitman delivered a scathing indictment of the dawning era of professional sport, complaining that wolves, snakes, and dogs had entered into the previously pristine, democratic National Pastime.

The story makes you wonder what the legendary American poet would have made of the spitball or the scuffball—or, for that matter, the 1919 Black Sox scandal.

In summary: Asking who "invented" the curveball is a little like asking who "wrote" an old folksong. Not for the first time in baseball's evaluation of its own early history, a decision was made by the Powers That Be to overlook a complex set of truths behind a gradual innovation that bears the mark of many hands—and steadfastly refuses to fit neatly into a single "creation" narrative. Cummings's election to the Hall of Fame says more about the remarkable human tendency to resolve doubts and questions by attaching stories to them than it does about the relative merits of the pitcher in question. (See also the entries relative to the "invention" of the game of baseball by Abner Doubleday [Myth 6] and Alexander Cartwright [Myth 4].)

MYTH 47

The Designated-Hitter Rule Was the Brainchild of Oakland A's Owner Charles O. Finley

For the purist the DH may be a pet peeve,
But it's older than most detractors believe.

Offense-hungry fans swear by it. Purist fans swear *at* it, arguing that it removes essential strategic questions from the game.

However you feel about the designated-hitter rule that allows another hitter to stand in for the pitcher, you can't ignore it—since 1973, it has been operating procedure in the American League. Some people think it shouldn't be, but it is.

With the notable exception of the National League, the DH has more or less taken over at all levels of professional baseball, and in recent years it has always played *some* role in the annual World Series. Following a number of years in which the pennant-winners played by differing rules in alternating seasons, the game's bigwigs decided, sensibly enough, to allow the home team's rules to prevail. The argument went like this: How fair is it to work for a decade to build or take part in a pennant-winning team—perhaps the only one of your career—and then have to play the entire

World Series by different rules from those your team was built around?

The designated-hitter rule, which provides offensive punch for the (typically weak-hitting) pitcher, means that statistics between the American and National Leagues don't quite match up, and haven't for years. A.L. team earned-run averages, and most team batting statistics, are always a little higher than their N.L. counterparts. In recent years, ballooning offensive statistics, most noticeable in the American League thanks to the DH, have prompted more than one distressed fan to ask: Why did the baseball gods listen to Oakland A's owner Charlie Finley when he first came up with this idea?

Well, Finley *didn't* come up with the idea, although he was certainly one of its most enthusiastic proponents. Fans of 1–0 and 2–1 games—contests that seem rarer now than ever, at least in the A.L.—may not like to admit it, but the idea of the designated hitter has a long pedigree, and whether you like it or hate it, the notion cannot be laid entirely at the feet of the late (and controversial) Oakland A's owner. It should be noted, however, that Finley also lobbied for baseball with Day-Glo balls and players whose only function was to run the bases. Go ahead and lay those ideas at his feet. Although the rest of organized baseball didn't seem to think much of the designated-runner idea, Finley ordered manager Alvin Dark to give the experiment a try, and thus launched the baseball career of Herb Washington, a sprinter who had never even played minor-league ball. Washington's sole job was to steal bases; he stole twenty-five of them and never played the field or came to bat. Unfortunately, his "safe" percentage (64 percent) was not high enough to justify a roster spot. Washington was cut in 1975; Finley continued to tinker with the notion of the designated runner, but it never caught on.

Odd-colored balls and nonhitting, nonfielding players

were pretty wild notions, and they were all Finley's, but the DH had been percolating for a while longer. Like, more than half a century.

Surprise, surprise: National League president John Heydler was the first to propose a rule allowing the pitcher's place to be filled by a nonfielding offensive player. Back in the 1920s, Heydler pointed (as most of the DH's supporters still do) to a hitting pitcher's near-universal status as an "automatic out," and to the fact that the pitcher's presence in the lineup tends to restrict the offensive action. (Self-described baseball purists, the author among them, don't much care, and would rather see the manager have to choose what to do when the pitcher's spot rolls around in the seventh inning of a tight, low-scoring game. But we're in the minority, and we know it.)

Although some National League owners were behind Heydler's idea, American League bigwigs vetoed the notion of a designated hitter. They argued that there was already enough offensive action—much of it, as it turned out, being supplied by a former pitcher named Babe Ruth, who seemed to have handled the challenges of the batter's box without too much trouble. Hey—for every rule, there's an exception, right?

Charles Finley was indeed the most noticeable mover and shaker behind the adoption of the designated-hitter rule in the early 1970s, but he was resurrecting an old idea whose time both had (in the A.L.) and had not (in the N.L.) come. This time, the two leagues took the opposite viewpoints on the merits of the designated hitter, but the change was nevertheless made in the American League.

The last A.L. team to win a pennant and world championship *without* a regular-season designated hitter was...(drum roll, please)...Finley's own 1972 Oakland A's. The DH rule was put into practice in 1973, smack in the middle of Finley's squad's three-year reign as the top team in the American League. During the World Series, however, the early-seventies A's were never able to take advantage of the rules change that had been so strongly associated with their flamboyant owner. Every game of the A's appearances in the 1973 series (against the New York Mets) and the 1974 series (against the Los Angeles Dodgers), was played under National League rules.

Beginning in 1976, the Series permitted designated hitters by means of an alternating-season system, under which the DH rule was only in effect in even-numbered years for Fall Classic play. That lasted until the 1986 Series, in which officials decreed that the DH rule would be observed in games played in the American League champion's home park, but not in games in which the National League's pennant-winners were the home team.

Whether you think the designated-hitter rule is a travesty that deprives thinking fans of another welcome chance to second-guess managers, or you think it adds more excitement to a game that runs the risk of seeming sedentary at times, the truth of the matter is that the designated-hitter rule is no recent innovation, and certainly not the result of a Charlie Finley brainstorm.

Let's remember the controversial Finley for his unique character, his relentless showmanship, and his many legitimate achivements within the game, among which which was the assembly of the great Oakland dynasty of the seventies: a three-time batch of world champions with attitude aplenty and grown-to-order handlebar mustaches.

And those green-and-gold uniforms, which *were* Finley's idea.

In summary: John Heydler, not Charles O. Finley, was the first major-league figure of note to propose the designated-hitter rule.

MYTH 46

The "Tinker-to-Evers-to-Chance" Infield Was the Premier Double-Play Combination of Its Era

Tinker-to-Evers-to-Chance sounds great,
But was their double-play total first-rate?

There is a submyth to deal with before we get to the main item on the agenda here. The correct title of the Franklin P. Adams poem that immortalized the Chicago Cubs' now-famous infield was *not* "Tinker-to-Evers-to-Chance"—it was "Baseball's Sad Lexicon." It should perhaps have been called the "Overrated Double-Play Combination."

No one is arguing that the infield that included shortstop Joe Tinker, second baseman Johnny Evers, and first baseman Frank Chance wasn't *good*. It certainly was that, and it was also innovative, resulting in new approaches to the hit-and-run play, the bunt, and the stolen base. It just didn't turn all that many double plays, but people tend to think that it did, thanks to Adams's poem—and the fact that all three players were inducted into the Hall of Fame in the same year (1946).

The trio's heyday came between 1903 and 1910—the latter years of which period were a good time for Cubs fans, who got to watch their team set up what seemed to be the beginnings of a dynasty. Tinker posted the best fielding

....

mark of any National League shortstop in 1906, 1908, and 1909. Evers made more putouts than any second baseman in his league (344) in 1906. Chance led senior circuit's first basemen in fielding in 1907 with a .992 mark. They were quite sharp on the field (as Giant Fred Merkle, the victim of Evers's putout in a memorable 1908 game, would certainly have attested).

The guys just didn't turn all that many double plays—at any rate, not enough to eclipse the National League teams against whom they were playing at the time.

For the record: Cincinnati, not the Cubs, led the league in team double plays in 1905. Pittsburgh, not the Cubs, led the league in team double plays in 1906. Boston, not the Cubs, led the league in team double plays in 1907 and 1908. Cincinnati, not the Cubs, led the league in team double plays in 1909. And Boston, not the Cubs, led the league in team double plays in 1910. Only Tinker ever led the league in double plays at his position, and he did that only once (in 1905).

Francis Adams composed his much-quoted poem in 1910, the last year the trio played together. It sounded pretty good then, and it sounds pretty good now, but the honored memory reserved for the double-play combination of which he wrote may have more to do with a fortuitous set of names than with the Chicago infield's superior knack for executing double plays.

All three men were tough, capable players. Player-manager Frank Chance—also known as "Husk" and the "Peerless Leader"—piloted the Chicago Cubs to the National League pennant during the team's (and the infield trio's) most celebrated period. Chance led the Cubs to first-place finishes in 1906, 1907, 1908, and 1910. His teams won the Series in 1907 and 1908. Chance had a lifetime 768–389 record as a Cubs manager, posting the best winning percentage (.664) in the history of that franchise. And at bat and on the basepaths, the young manager was quite capable of emerging as a force to be reckoned with. He led the National League in stolen bases with 57 in 1906, and hit .319. In the 1908 World Series, Chance hit at a .421 clip, the best batting average on either side.

The careers of Johnny Evers (who won the Most Valuable Player award in 1914) and Joe Tinker (who stole home twice in one game in 1910) were marred by a long-standing feud between the two that was apparently the result of a 1905 argument over cabfare. Evers and Tinker didn't speak to each other for years, but were reconciled in 1938, during the World Series that year that boasted an appearance by their old team, the Chicago Cubs.

All three members of the celebrated infield combination eventually served as managers of the Chicago Cubs.

In summary: It may have sounded magnificent in a poem— better, no doubt, than "Wagner-to-Ritchey-to-Nealon" (except to Pittsburgh fans of the era)—but the celebrated threesome deserves to be remembered for things other than their ability to turn twin killings more prodigiously than anyone of their time. They didn't.

MYTH 45

Lou Boudreau Introduced the Defensive "Shift"

Yes, Boudreau gave fielders some strange things to do,
But the first "shift" predates that of Cleveland's man Lou.

During the 1946 season, Boston slugger Ted Williams found himself staring at a strange defensive alignment during a game against the Indians.

Cleveland skipper Lou Boudreau, tired of watching Williams drive hits to the right, had decided to reposition his fielders. He'd ordered his third baseman to move closer to the shortstop, and he positioned the rest of the infield in such a way that everyone occupied a zone between first base and a little bit beyond second. In the outfield, too, everyone moved over to the right.

In other words, the left side of the playing field was more or less unguarded. Williams's bread-and-butter right side, however, was choked with fielders.

The Red Sox star, who had recently hit three home runs in a single game against Cleveland, laughed and waited for the umpire to tell the Indians to resume their normal positions. But it was no joke. As Boudreau knew, there is no clause in the rule book stating *where* the seven nonbattery defensive players must be stationed. All they must do is show up on the field . . . somewhere. If Cleveland had wanted to position one man on the mound, one behind the plate, and seven clustered near first base, it could have done so.

Ted Williams, as the Cleveland skipper knew, was a stubborn man. The great left-handed hitter could easily have shifted *in response* to the shift, perhaps by hitting something down the third-base line. But he didn't. (He was quoted as saying that trying to take advantage of the shift in this way would have been "a mark of weakness.") Williams didn't alter his hitting style against the shift. And the results won Boudreau a good deal of press coverage. Other American League teams eventually tried the shift, and Williams usually—but not always—kept pounding the ball to the right side.

St. Louis employed the "shift" in the 1946 World Series against Boston, in which Williams hit only .200. The Cardinals won.

But did Boudreau really invent the daring defensive shift?

It turns out that the stunt was a baseball gimmick of long standing, having been used in both the American and National leagues as far back as 1922. Oddly the victims at the plate were also named Williams, one in each league. In the A.L., a shift similar to Boudreau's was tried against outfielder Ken Williams of the Browns (who nevertheless posted a .332 average that year). In the N.L., the victim was Cy Williams, an outfielder for the Phillies (who hit .308 for the season). Did Boudreau know about the earlier defensive shifts? Whether or not he did, he can't be credited as the originator of the strategy.

Ted Williams hit .342 during the regular season in 1946, shift or no shift. Although the defensive realignment that caught on for a time in the American League may have cost Williams some points on his batting average, it didn't keep him from fashioning the kind of career dreams are made of. The Splendid Splinter's later years boasted, among many other highlights, a sparkling .388 average posted in 1957, when he was *thirty-nine years old*, and a legendary home run in the last at-bat of his career in 1960.

As for Boudreau, he went on to a glorious 1948 season in which he hit .355, knocked in 106 runs, posted the best fielding average of any starting shortstop in the league, *and* piloted his team to the pennant. The Indians took the flag by beating the Red Sox in a one-game playoff at season's end. Under the crafty, relentless Boudreau's guidance, the Tribe put down the Boston Braves in the Fall Classic that year, 4 games to 2. There have been players who've had better years, and there have been managers who've had better years, but there may well never have been one man who did both jobs at the same time as well as Lou Boudreau did in 1948.

In summary: Whether you call it the "Williams Shift" or the "Boudreau Shift," what the Cleveland manager pulled against Teddy Ballgame was not a recent innovation.

MYTH 44

The First World Series Was Played in 1903

The Series predated the A.L., I swear;
It was also an A.A. and N.L. affair!

When a strike ended the 1994 season prematurely, baseball fans were left without a clear champion for the first time since 1904, when the National League champions refused to play the American League champions. Many reporters referred to the previous year's World Series—the 1903 set, in which the Boston Pilgrims defeated the Pittsburgh Pirates—as the "first" World Series.

But the World Series was initially a series of games between the National League champions and the American Association champions. The American Association set up shop as a major league in 1882—nineteen years before the American League's first season, in 1901—and lasted until 1891.

Between the years 1884 and 1890, the two leagues squared off in end-of-season competition that crowned championship squads much as the modern World Series does, with the significant exception that some of the series from these years ended in ties, and not all of the contests were best-of-seven affairs. (Not even twentieth-century World Series have always been maximum-seven-game contests; the 1921 Series, for instance, was a best-of-nine match.) According to Charles C. Alexander's fine book *Our Game: An American Baseball History*, the 1884 postseason series between the Providence Grays of the National League and the New York Metropolitans of the American Association, "was billed as the first 'World's Championship Series,'—or simply 'World Series.'" Providence won, three games to none. (An 1882 series had been called off with the American Association and National League champions tied at one game apiece.)

National League teams won the Series in 1887, 1888, and 1889. American Association teams won the Series in 1885 and 1886. The 1895 and 1890 Series ended in ties.

In 1891, the two leagues, engaged in a series of bitter turf wars, did not mount a World Series. By 1892, the American Association was defunct, four of its teams having been absorbed by the National League. This meant that, where there previously had been two major leagues, there now was only one. But just as the modern-day National Football League concludes its year with postseason play that crowns a world champion, without that champion encountering a team from a rival league, so the National League of a century ago structured an end-of-season championship format that allowed its best teams to play for the title "best team in baseball."

For a number of years in the 1890s, a series of intraleague contests known as the Temple Cup games took place between the first- and second-place National League teams. The name was chosen in honor of the Pittsburgh sportsman William Temple, president of the Pirates, who donated the trophy for which the teams played. The first team to win three of the end-of-season series would gain permanent ownership of the cup.

Although the Temple Cup games were apparently not as closely watched as earlier postseason contests, these games were best-four-out-of-seven affairs that crowned baseball's champions for the year. The New York Giants took the first set of games for the cup in 1894. The Baltimore Orioles (the "old" National League team that bears the same name as, but is not connected to, the current American League Baltimore franchise) took the championship four games to one in 1897, the final year of Temple Cup play.

In summary: Although the first World Series between the American and National Leagues indeed took place in 1903, the first World Series *ever* did not.

MYTH 43

Brooklyn Dodger Babe Herman Tripled Into a Triple Play

The sight of three men on a base may be funny,
But triples and triple plays? Want to bet money?

Lots of baseball fans have heard—and laughed at—the story of how inept baserunning by Brooklyn's Babe Herman resulted in a triple that turned into a triple play in the mid-twenties. It could only happen to the Bums of that era, right?

It makes a great story. But it didn't happen. Not that that's stopped people from circulating this classic baseball nonevent. Some people pass along the version of the story in which Herman tripled into a double play. That's closer to the truth, but still not correct.

Certainly something very bizarre *did* happen during the game in question. But it's not what people think happened. If you're ever short on cash in a bar, you may be able to pick up some quick dough on this one.

Fact check. August 15, 1926: The Dodgers were hosting the Boston Braves, and Brooklyn was trailing, 1–0, in the bottom of the seventh inning. Johnny Butler singled for Brooklyn; Hank DeBerry then doubled, scoring Butler. Tie game. Pitcher Dazzy Vance singled. Chick Fewster drew a walk, loading the bases.

A pitching change ensued; the next batter, Merwin Jacobson, popped out.

That's right. He popped out. One official, unrevokable out. That leaves two up for grabs. Which brings us to Babe Herman.

Herman took his place in the batter's box. He hit a drive to right field.

The man on third, DeBerry, scored with no difficulty.

Vance, the man on second, found himself staring at an apprentice third-base coach (Brooklyn's reserve catcher) whose signs seem to have betrayed a measure of uncertainty. Vance took no chances and waited for the ball to fall for a hit (which it did) before heading for third.

Fewster, the man on first, confident Herman's drive would fall safely, ran like lightning.

For his part, Herman ran pretty confidently too, but he doesn't seem to have bothered to look at any of his companions on the basepath.

Vance made a big turn at third, but then opted to head back to the bag rather than attempt to score. That's when things got very strange.

Fewster, who had barreled around second, was heading into third when he saw Vance there. He stopped short. The less-than-observant Herman then passed the baserunner in front of him—Fewster—and slid with gusto into third base, the base occupied by Vance, the runner in front of *Fewster*.

With this memorable piece of baserunning Herman had made the second out of the inning. (A runner who passes another on the basepaths is automatically out.) He had only made the first out of the *play* however. There was another to follow; Fewster was trapped in a surrealistic game of tag that concluded with his being called out in, of all places, right field. That third out ended the inning.

Herman, who was out the moment he passed Fewster, never made it safely to third, so he can hardly be credited with a triple. And since there was already one out, a triple play would have been, well, excessive.

It was a weird enough sequence already.

By the way, the Dodgers won. But nobody remembers *that*. Instead, the day gave rise to the endlessly repeated joke in which one wag observes that the Dodgers have managed to get three men on base—and his companion asks, "Really? Which one?"

As for Herman, he led the National League in errors at first base in 1927, and in the outfield in 1928. He persistently denied the vicious story that he had once been beaned in the outfield by an oncoming fly ball.

Herman's exploits as a hitter make him look a lot better than his oft-recounted misadventures in the field or on the basepaths. He hit for the cycle—single, double, triple, and homer in the same game—three times, and posted a lifetime .324 batting average. In 1930, Herman hit for a staggering .393 season average, but he didn't win the batting title. That honor went to Bill Terry of the Giants, who stroked .401 that year, and thus became the last National Leaguer to hit .400 or better.

In summary: It was a double play, not a triple play. The tale has often been amended in the retelling over the years to allow all three baserunners to be called out at third base. One might make an argument that this would only have been poetic justice, but the fact remains there was one out at the time Herman strode to the plate, that Herman was out before he made it to third, and that he was credited with a double, not a triple.

MYTH 42

The Professional Ban on Hiring Black Players Was an Informal "Gentleman's Agreement" That Was Never Committed to Writing

The shame of the game of baseball's no joke,
'Twas more than a nod and a wink: It was spoke!

More than one baseball scribe has passed along the contention that the exclusion of blacks from organized baseball was entirely an informal matter, something that was independently observed among various club officials at various levels of the game. It's not true.

Even if the case can be made that the big leagues never put a prohibition of black players into writing for public review, the same cannot be said of the minor leagues. The oldest minor league in America, the International League, passed a formal measure to exclude black players, in July of 1887. By helping to solidify the color line in the minor leagues, the I.L. took a step that made it much easier to preserve the later fiction that big-league baseball executives never *actively* took steps to prohibit blacks from playing; they just went with the flow. How, baseball bigwigs seemed to be asking, were *they* supposed to control what players the

....

minor leagues developed? And where else were most big-leaguers supposed to come from, if not the minor leagues?

Whether a formal ban on black players at the major-league level existed depends on how you define "formal." If we take the word to mean "officially and openly pronounced," then, no, major-league officials never admitted their policy of discrimination publicly, and never passed a measure restricting clubs from hiring whomever they pleased. This fact was frequently, and hypocritically, pressed into service by top baseball men, including Commissioner Judge Kenesaw Mountain Landis. In 1943, Landis told the world that each individual major-league club was "entirely free to employ Negro players to any and all extent it pleases. The matter is solely for each club's decision, without restriction whatsoever."

If we define "formal" as "pursued as a matter of established practice and commonly recognized standards," however, the idea that big-league baseball's ban on black players was "informal" quickly becomes absurd. In particular, Landis's contention that each club was free to act as it saw fit in terms of hiring is patent nonsense. As former commissioner Happy Chandler—the man who gave Branch Rickey approval to bring up Jackie Robinson—recalled it in his eighties, "Any time there was a hint of a black player being brought into the game, Landis had a standard answer—I've read the minutes of the meetings—Landis said, 'I've said everything that's going to be said on that subject. The answer is no.' Then he would move on to new business."

Even the contention that big-league baseball never committed its racist guidelines to paper is problematic. A secret 1946 report on the controversial subject of integration in baseball was apparently prepared by a group of owners, together with the presidents of the American and National leagues. It recommended that black players continue to be excluded from big-league play. Because of the sensitive nature of the document, all copies were supposedly collected and destroyed after its initial circulation. Some have argued that a copy still exists *somewhere*, but it has yet to surface. If the document ever does materialize, it should be openly acknowledged by big-league baseball's current leadership (if such it can be called) for what it is: long-suppressed evidence of morally indefensible cynicism, connivance with racial hatred, dishonesty toward the fans of the game...and an example that must never be followed again.

See Joel Zoss and John Bowman's fine book *Diamonds in the Rough* for a more detailed discussion of the shameful way big-league baseball maintained the color line by means of its decisions at the very highest levels.

In summary: Organized baseball's first exclusion of black players was on paper, and meant for public review, in 1887. Later attempts to maintain the fantasy that no top-level policy of exclusion existed in the big leagues were insults to the intelligence of fans and players. This policy *did* exist, and at the highest levels, but the Powers That Be lacked the courage to express them openly. Baseball Commissioner Kenesaw Mountain Landis, who assumed absolute (and often tyrannical) authority over major league baseball in 1920 after the Black Sox scandal rocked it to its foundations, bears much of the responsibility for the maintenance of the game's publicly unspoken, but nevertheless firmly entrenched, policy of racial discrimination.

MYTH 41

Ty Cobb Won the 1910 American League Batting Title

If nice guys go last, as da Bum had it reckoned,
It's great when a jerk somehow ends up second.

Ruthless, sociopathic, racist, violent, abusive, and a hell of a player, Ty Cobb was probably the most feared man in the history of baseball.

We are talking here about a man who had some pretty serious social adjustment problems, and who would almost certainly have landed in jail—or at the very least have been banned from the game—if he'd played in modern times. (In Cleveland, Cobb once knifed a black watchman who had asked him who he was; the Detroit star hightailed it out of town and only narrowly avoided arrest.)

We are also talking about a man who hit .323 at the age of forty-one. Late in his career or early in his career, Cobb was a certifiable hit machine. His ferocious approach to the game earned him a batting title in 1907, at the tender age of twenty.

In his long and illustrious career, the left-handed-hitting Cobb led the league in hits eight times, runs scored five times, doubles three times, triples four times, and stolen bases six times. He hit under .300 only once—during his rookie season—and posted season averages over .380 nine times. Of those nine seasons, three saw Cobb finish up at .400 or better. He wrapped up his twenty-four-year career with the highest lifetime batting average anyone has ever had, and likely ever will have: .367. During those twenty-four years, he was able to scoop up a total of twelve hitting championships.

But later baseball scholarship has revealed that one of those championships was a title he did not deserve. Cobb got it anyway. (Something tells me the feisty misanthrope probably wouldn't have wanted it any other way.)

In 1910, Cobb found himself in a nip-and-tuck hitting battle with Cleveland's popular Napoleon Lajoie—one of the most successful right-handed hitters of the dead-ball era, and a strong candidate for the honor of top second baseman of all time. Although Cobb had won the last three batting titles in a row, Lajoie was taking him on with renewed vigor in 1910, due in part to a change in the Cleveland infielder's job description.

At the start of the season, Lajoie had checked in as a player only, rather than as Cleveland's player-manager, a role he had performed for the preceding five years. Cleveland had finished fourth, fifth, third, fourth, second, and sixth during Lajoie's tenure as manager, and the second baseman felt his dual job had both undercut his own performance at the plate and damaged his team's chances in the race for the American League pennant.

As it happened, neither Lajoie's team nor Cobb's was able to come close to the soaring Philadelphia Athletics as the 1910 season moved toward its conclusion, but Lajoie's personal average had indeed climbed, seemingly as a result of his decision to focus on his own performance and leave the managing to new skipper Deacon McGuire. Lajoie had failed to hit .300 during the 1907 and 1908 seasons, and he had finished 53 points behind Cobb in the batting race in 1909. But the Cleveland star was now putting together one of his very best seasons at the plate, hitting in the .380 range as the season entered its final week.

It was clear that one of the two men was going to win the batting crown, and most of the baseball world was rooting for Lajoie, who was not only a superb player, but also had the advantage of coming across as something other than a maniac. At stake was a gleaming new motorcar from the Chalmers Motor Company.

At season's end, newspapers reported that Cobb had bested Lajoie by a single percentage point, .385 to .384. The race was a controversial one; a St. Louis player had been accused of playing deep, under instruction from both his coach and manager, in order to benefit Lajoie.

When the dust settled, though, American League president Ban Johnson had pronounced that Cobb had won the race. The Chalmers people, evidently in reaction to the tightness of the finish, gave both men cars. (Cobb immediately sold his, infuriating the president of the company.)

Cobb, .385. Lajoie, .384 And so it stood for decades.

However...

In 1981, the *Sporting News* revealed research that indicated that Lajoie had won the batting title after all. The Georgia Peach, it turned out, had been credited *twice* with a 2-for-3 game, and two hitless times at bat had been omitted from his yearly totals. Lajoie's numbers were reviewed closely, as well—and the long-delayed final, final, *final* result of the 1910 batting contest is now regarded as follows:

Lajoie .383. Cobb, .382.

But hey, he still got the car. Or, at any rate, a check.

In summary: It's a case of delayed accounting, yes, and there's certainly no suggestion here that the 1910 errors in addition are the only ones lurking in the books. But this tight batting race was one that had a murky finish anyway, and the ledger review, whether or not it was overdue, seems to have been justified. The best and the brightest have now weighed in on Lajoie's side: Scratch those five at-bats and two hits from 1910 and give the posthumous honors to Nap. Ty can afford an accurate count.

MYTH 40

Pete Gray Was the First Handicapped Major-Leaguer

The Browns brought him up, and he knew how to play,
But Gray wasn't the first of his kind—no way.

There have not been many disabled players in the major leagues—although in our day pitcher Jim Abbott has certainly made his mark.

Many people believe that the first handicapped big-league ballplayer was the St. Louis Browns' outfielder Pete Gray. Gray, who had only one arm, was brought up to the (wartime) major leagues in 1945, and he played 77 games for the St. Louis Browns—who were, as the season began, baseball's reigning world champions. Gray had lost his arm as a child in a truck accident, and he was no fluke. He was a good hitter, a daring runner, and a surprisingly capable outfielder; he had developed a defensive technique that allowed him to make a catch, tuck his glove under the stump of his missing right arm, roll the ball across his chest, and throw back to the infield. To many observers, it all looked as natural as water over a pebble.

After a semipro career that won him fame in his native Pennsylvania and in Brooklyn, Gray broke into pro baseball in 1942, posting a strong .381 average for the Three Rivers team in the Canadian-American League. In 1943, he played an entire season with Memphis in the Southern League, batting .289. The next year, he earned headlines by hitting .333 for Memphis and stealing 68 bases. He was named the Most Valuable Player in the Southern League for 1944.

The truth is, however, that at the time of his stint on the war-depleted Browns roster, Gray was neither the first, nor the most successful, handicapped player in the big leagues.

Between the years 1882 and 1887, Hugh "One Arm" Daily pitched for the National League, the Union Association, and the American Association. He threw for Cleveland in 1883, compiling a 23–19 record and tossing a no-hitter against Philadelphia. The next year, he led the Union Association in strikeouts. Daily's career was less notable in its last few years, but he did post three strong seasons, and he closed out his career with a lifetime 3.05 earned-run average. We are told that Daily fielded by means of a pad attached to one forearm that he used to knock down batted balls.

Other handicapped players to precede Gray include pitcher Luther Taylor and outfielder William Hoy, both of whom were deaf-mutes. Taylor won 21 games for the New York Giants in 1904, and posted a total of 112 victories over nineteen years. Hoy led the National League in stolen bases in 1888, and fashioned a fourteen-year big-league career in which he played in at least 100 games for all but his last season. He hit over .300 three times, and finished up with a lifetime batting average of .288.

Pete Gray's appearance in the major leagues was, primarily, a media event. He posted a .218 batting average and did not return when the conclusion of wartime commitments permitted many of baseball's enlisted men to resume their jobs on the field. Unlike Daily, Taylor, and Hoy, Gray was not able to make a go of it in the major leagues for an extended period.

In summary: Although Gray may have been the most prominent handicapped major-league ballplayer of his day, he was definitely not the first.

MYTH 39

Bill Buckner's Error Blew the Red Sox Lead in the Sixth Game of the 1986 World Series

The most fateful of grounders? Yes, but please note:
The '86 Red Sox had more than one goat.

God help the player upon whom a media tornado descends.

If you were to gather together a group of 100 baseball fans and ask all of them, "Who's the man most responsible for the collapse of the Boston Red Sox in the sixth game of the 1986 World Series?" odds are that at least 95 would respond, "Bill Buckner." Perhaps all 100 would cite Buckner as the man who cost Boston the title that they came within a whisker of winning in 1986.

We all watch TV. We all listen to radio. We've all seen and heard (and seen and heard and seen and heard) the infamous play that deprived the Red Sox of their first World Series championship since 1918, so we all know that if Buckner had made the play at first base, if he had only been able to handle Mookie Wilson's fateful ground ball in the tenth inning, then the Red Sox would have won the game, and the Series.

Well, we're all wrong. What's more, some of us—I'm thinking here of intelligent sportswriters and broadcasters who really do know better—*know* this account is wrong, and don't say anything. And that's a shame.

We've hung the career-defining horns of the "World Series goat" on a solid player who won the 1980 National League batting title with a .324 average, led his league in doubles twice, and played all 162 games at first base in 1985. We've taken everything Bill Buckner worked for and accomplished over a memorable major-league career and turned it into a joke—which might be fine, except that this particular joke doesn't reflect all the facts. We've done this because we like shorthand. We've done it because it was easy to do, and maybe even a little bit enjoyable. We've done it because there doesn't seem to be much wrong with oversimplifying things, to succumbing to the modern mania for holding one person accountable for disaster, lest sports talk-show jocks have one less gag line to work with. We've messed up a good man's life because we can't be bothered with a (moderately) complex set of facts.

The fault lies not in ourselves, or at least not completely in ourselves, but in the media's penchant for drama. The film clip (and the audio track) of Buckner blowing that ground ball is certainly *dramatic*. It's impossible to ignore. It's short. It's sweet. (Unless you're from Boston, in which case it's agonizing, but I digress.) The few seconds of Buckner muffing that ground ball represent an easy way to summarize the 1986 World Series if you only have an instant in which to do so.

Easy. But not entirely accurate.

Bill Buckner's error may have ended the game, but it did *not* blow the lead the Boston Red Sox had built going into the bottom of the tenth inning. Relief pitchers Calvin Schiraldi and Bob Stanley did that job, and it is one of the tragic ironies of the game that their shortcomings on this score have been allowed to slip into the "pesky detail" category, *because their errors were more numerous and more severe and more intricate than Buckner's,* and therefore more difficult to encapsulate in a short film or audio clip. The decline of the national attention span has its costs, and Bill Buckner has paid it—and probably will continue to pay it for the rest of his life.

Buckner's moment of agony made for the most compelling—and concise—bit of televised human drama associated with the sixth game, and so his error was what we saw (and still see) over and over in evaluations of the game. But Buckner didn't blow the two-run lead that should have held up in the bottom of the tenth. He merely cost the Red Sox the chance to try to put the game back together in the eleventh. Heaven knows it was a play Buckner would have loved dearly to do over, but the fielding lapse was only the last of the team's hideous exercises in self-destruction that inning, and by no means the worst of the lot.

The sequence of the fateful inning was as follows: Calvin Schiraldi got Mets batters Wally Backman and Keith Hernandez out. The Red Sox were thus an out away from triumph when Gary Carter singled to left field. Then pinch-hitter Kevin Mitchell singled to center. Then Ray Knight came up to bat; Schiraldi got two strikes on him—agonizingly close to the championship—but then yielded a single to center. Carter scored. It was a one-run game. Sox skipper John McNamara made his way to the mound, then signaled for right-hander Bob Stanley.

All Stanley had to do was get one guy out. But then again, for the last three batters, that was all Schiraldi had had to do.

Mookie Wilson was waiting for Stanley at the plate.

If there were any justice in this insane world of ours, it would be the whole of Wilson's long, surrealistic at-bat that sportscasters would play when they discussed the collapse of the Red Sox in the sixth game. But there is no justice, and we do live in an era of slogans and condensations and hype.

So we don't sit through repeated broadcasts of Stanley's working Wilson to an 0–2 count, then missing outside by a hair, then throwing an inside pitch that utterly mystified catcher Rich Gedman and scooted past him, allowing the tying run to score.

It went into the books as a wild pitch. Wilson fouled off a series of pitches, as though intent on prolonging the strange spectacle. On Stanley's tenth pitch, Wilson stroked a ground ball toward Buckner. The rest, as they say, is history.

The Boston Red Sox, who had taken a 3–2 lead in games over the heavily favored Mets, and whose pitchers had had thirteen chances to deliver the strike that would have clinched the championship, were beaten. The game had been in the bag, but it wasn't Bill Buckner who changed that. Still, Buckner's miscue made for great television—and harping on his (underserved) status as the main cause of the Boston collapse became a kind of media frenzy in the weeks and months and years that followed.

It was a damn shame, and he deserved better.

In summary: Bill Buckner deserved a break in 1986, and he deserves one today. If he is to be consigned to the corner of baseball hell occupied by the game's legendary goats—a position that even a cursory examination of the game in question simply doesn't support—then he should, at the very least, be accompanied thence by Messrs. Schiraldi and Stanley.

MYTH 38

The 1919 Chicago White Sox Won Their "Black Sox" Nickname From the Gambling Scandal That Enveloped Them

What's in a name? There are plenty of theories.
But "Black Sox" had nothing to do with the Series.

The 1919 Chicago White Sox may well have been one of the great teams in baseball history, but their play in the infamous World Series of that year deprived them of the chance to prove it. The name by which we now know them, however—the "Black Sox"—did not originate because of the team's involvement with unsavory gamblers. And even though the team's owner had no role in the decision to toss the Series, the "Black Sox" name *did* arise out of *his* unsavory practices.

Some exposition is probably in order for those unfamiliar with the scandal. After the White Sox emerged as heavy favorites to defeat the Cincinnati Reds in the 1919 Series, discontented Chicago first baseman Chick Gandil's connections with gambling figures Joseph "Sport" Sullivan, Abe Attell, and Billy Maharg led to an attempt to throw the Series. A number of other players, including star pitcher Eddie Cicotte (who had posted 28 wins and a microscopic 1.53 earned-run average in 1917), went along with the fix.

The 5–1 odds favoring Chicago meant that the final result of the Series—an upset Cincinnati win—resulted in huge payouts to those betting on the Reds.

Gambling was nothing new to the sport of baseball—it had been one of the reasons behind the self-destruction of the National Association—but fixing a World Series was unprecedented. When word got out about what had happened, the national media had a field day.

The scandal that ended the careers of eight Chicago players (Gandil, Cicotte, Joe Jackson, Lefty Williams, Hap Felsch, Swede Risberg, Fred McMullin, and Buck Weaver) broke during the 1920 season; when it did, the team took on the name "Black Sox," and it threatened not only the players involved, but the very foundations of major-league baseball. If more had been made at the time of the genesis of that ominous "Black Sox" nickname, a larger measure of shame for the events leading up to 1919 would perhaps have been laid at the feet of the man who most deserved it: owner Charles Comiskey.

Comiskey was unspeakably, incomprehensibly cheap, and this was made all the more pathetic by his status as a former player, a man who knew full well what baseball players had to go through to make ends meet. (Comiskey, who played first base, appears to have helped to popularize the practice of playing defense without keeping a foot on the bag.) He played for, and managed, the St. Louis Browns of the American Association, leading them to four championships in four years. But he won his greatest renown as an owner, rather than as a player or a manager. And he was so tight with cash that he secured the undying enmity of many of his best players, including, notably, Gandil and Cicotte.

As the Sox' ace pitcher prepared for his upcoming games against the Reds, he was coming off a superb year in 1919 (he went 29–7 in that fateful season), but he knew that, at thirty-five, he was looking at the end of a magnificent career, and he knew, too, that he was doing so without much money in the bank. Comiskey had steadfastly refused to pay his star pitcher anything remotely resembling what he was worth. In the days before free agency, that meant Cicotte faced three options: throw games, get out of baseball, or keep working on management's terms. In the 1919 World Series, he made his choice.

Yet the pressures that led to the 1919 scandal had been building for some time. Exactly how bad "management's terms" had been during the time Cicotte and the others were struggling under Comiskey's penurious management style can be glimpsed in the White Sox team policy for laundering uniforms in 1918, the year before the fateful Series. Comiskey refused to allocate cash to keep the team's uniforms clean. They played in visibly soiled ones and dubbed themselves the "Black Sox."

Two years later, in 1920, when the details of the 1919 scandal became public knowledge, the baseball world went into a coma and only repeated doses of Babe Ruth and Commissioner Kenesaw Mountain Landis could revive it. The participants in the scheme were ruined, and perhaps the city of Chicago's dreams of baseball glory as well. Bad karma alert: No team from Chicago, as of this writing, has won a World Series since the 1919 squad's fall.

Ironically, the "Black Sox" name, coined in protest, came to haunt the eight men who had been linked to the gambling scheme (and who did not, incidentally, secure their dreamed-of financial security). The man the name should have haunted was Charles Comiskey. Cicotte and the others were acquitted of criminal charges on technicalities, but were banned from baseball for life.

The headline shorthand inspired by the foul uniforms White Sox players had had to put up with said more about the genesis of the scandal than most people realized. But in the end, it was the players, rather than Comiskey, who suffered most.

Charles Comiskey was elected to baseball's Hall of Fame in 1939.

In summary: Comiskey's "frugal" ways were the cause of the name—and the later scandal—that has haunted the game of baseball for seventy-plus years.

MYTH 37

George Brett Won the 1976 American League Batting Title Without Divine Intervention

A single at-bat makes the difference some years,
But an out that's a hit? That's the case, it appears.

Okay, okay, if you pull out that massive copy of the *Baseball Encyclopedia* and check page 524, you will see Brett's name listed atop the entries for "Batting Average" in the end-of-season summary for 1976. There's the name: "G. Brett, KC / .333" right at the top of the column. But who's content to let pious legalisms carry the day when moral issues are at stake?

Check the second line. There you will see the entry "H. McRae, KC / .332"—and thereby hangs a tale.

No, Brett didn't bribe the editors of the *Encyclopedia*. He didn't engage in any skullduggery at all. The skullduggery—or at any rate, something that *looked* an awful lot like skullduggery—found him.

On the final day of the 1976 season, Brett was engaged in a tight battle with his teammate Hal McRae for the American League batting title. In his final at-bat, Brett hit a fly ball toward Minnesota outfielder Steve Brye that looked routine to some people—but not, evidently, to Brye, who, to all appearances, let it fall for a hit! The result: an inside-the-park home run. Brett's average inched up to .333, while McRae stayed a notch below at .332.

After the game, Brye made some strange remarks about Brett deserving the batting title more because he was a third baseman, not a designated hitter. How much is to be read into all this? It's hard to say, but a general consensus that Brye gave Brett's fly less than his personal best has emerged. When batting titles are on the line, bizarre things have been known to happen.

McRae finished his career with a .290 batting average, and never won a batting title. The *Sporting News* thrice named McRae Designated Hitter of the Year. He batted better than .300 six times and twice led the American League in doubles. The 1976 season, however, was his strongest overall year as a batter. Years later, his son Brian McRae played for the Royals, who at the time were being managed by...Hal McRae.

Brett posted a sizzling .390 average in 1980, the highest since Ted Williams's legendary .406 in 1941. He also copped the 1990 batting crown, with a .329 average—at the age of thirty-seven! That's three titles for Brett, two of them remarkable, and one of them...maybe a little less remarkable.

For an account of another controversial batting race—one that took decades to straighten out—see entry 41, which describes the legendary 1910 battle between Nap Lajoie and Mr. Personality, Ty Cobb.

In summary: Take the controversial hit away from Brett, and the 1976 title goes to McRae. Me, I put a little whiteout in my copy of the *Baseball Encyclopedia*, deleted and rewrote the first two lines, and gave McRae the crown. You may want to try it yourself. But be forewarned, you have to write *really* small.

MYTH 36

Nobody Hit Significant Numbers of Home Runs During the Pre-Ruth Era

"Mr. Round-tripper"? Babe earned it, of course.
But more than one man was a four-bagger force.

Before Babe Ruth emerged as a power hitter nonpareil, major-league baseball was most noticeable for (pick one):

(a) A seemingly unending series of low-scoring games.

(b) A complete absence of home-run champions who stroked more than, say, ten or twelve round-trippers in a single year.

(c) The failure of the home run to secure much in the way of strategic advantage to teams who somehow managed to lead the league in the generally over-looked category.

(d) All of the above.

Aren't you at least *tempted* to pick (d)? If you choose that answer, though, you're not taking into account, for instance, Philadelphia's 12–5 thrashing of the Chicago Cubs in the third game of the 1910 World Series, a game keyed by Danny Murphy's three-run blast; any number of home run champions who posted impressive (if not exactly Babe-like) sea-

47

son totals; and teams like the 1915 Phillies, whose league-leading home-run totals appear to have been keys to their success.

To read many baseball histories, you'd think that Babe Ruth more or less invented the home run. Would it surprise you to learn that there were as many home runs (three) hit in the five-game 1913 World Series as there were in the five-game 1922 World Series?

The accepted line sounds something like the following: People *kept track* of home runs before Ruth made his debut as an everyday player, but round-trippers were an anomaly, the kind of rare occurrence that showed up, at the end of the year, perhaps eight to twelve times in the statistics of the leading hitter in the category.

The implication: With Ruth's mark of 29 home runs in 1919 (the first year he played over a hundred games as a nonpitcher) baseball entered its maturity, offensively speaking, because no one had ever come close to hitting that many in a single season before.

Wrong.

Sometimes the end-of-year home run leaders during the pre-Ruth era checked in with numbers that look pretty scrawny by modern (i.e., post-1919) standards. But every once in a while, the league leader looked pretty darned good, even by contemporary standards—maybe not Ruthian, but not microscopic by any stretch of the imagination. In other words, the league leaders *didn't* always post home-run totals in the 8-to-15 range. Whether the reasons were the peculiar configurations of home ballparks, the greater ability of the athletes in question, or some elusive influence prevalent primarily among batters in the National League, the following men posted some pretty impressive home-run totals before Ruth came along:

• Ned Williamson (Chicago, N.L., 1884) 27

- Buck Freeman (Washington, N.L., 1899) 25
- Gavvy Cravath (Philadelphia, N.L., 1915) 20
- Wildfire Schulte (Chicago, N.L., 1911) 21
- Sam Thompson (Philadelphia, N.L., 1889) 20
- Ed Delahanty (Philadelphia, N.L., 1893) 19

Was every year like this? No. But *some* years were, and that's worth knowing.

Ruth *did* revolutionize the offensive game when he moved into the outfield and became an everyday player. But he wasn't the first person to hit a significant number of home runs in the major leagues.

In summary: No one can seriously dispute that Babe Ruth— the outfielder—was the player baseball needed in the early twenties, or that he did things that no one else had ever dreamed of doing before with a baseball bat. Yet he was not the first man to break through to the mid-to-high twenties in terms of yearly home run production, which is the impression many a writer has left.

MYTH 35

Bo Jackson Was the First Player to Boast Simultaneous Careers in Both Major-League Baseball and the National Football League

Bo was the player who handled it all?
Yeah, in ad campaigns, media, and the short haul.

When Bo Jackson decided to do double duty for the football Raiders and baseball Royals in the late 1980s, he unleashed a media and merchandising juggernaut. The storm of attention gave a lot of people the impression that Jackson's undertaking was unprecedented. It wasn't.

Prior to World War II, there were no fewer than twenty-one players who played both sports on the big-league level, not for the glory or the endorsements, but for a more old-fashioned reason: to make ends meet. In the 1920s and 1930s, many big-league ball players (Chuck Dressen, Tom Whelan, and Ernie Vick, to name only three) put in off-season duty with the NFL. This is not for a minute to suggest that performing at the top level in both sports is easy (or wise). But it is worth noting that the extravagant endorsement projects that came Jackson's—and more recently Deion Sanders's—way would have raised more than a few eyebrows on the part of some supremely dedicated prewar athletes. And although both games have changed over the years, it's worth remembering that these "double threats" put in their time with the NFL at a time when doing so was a lightly padded (and occasionally bloody) affair. Considerable physical resilience—and personal courage—must have been a requirement for those who opted to compete simultaneously in the world of professional football and major-league baseball during this period.

After the Second World War, simultaneous participation in both sports became much less common. Note, however, the schedule of Tom Brown, an outfielder who logged 61 games with the Washington Senators in 1963—and earned a roster spot with the Green Bay Packers in 1964. (Brown was also a member of the 1966 Packer squad that won the first Super Bowl.)

As for Jackson, he left his most memorable mark in the categories of media hype and commercial endorsements rather than in sustained onfield baseball performance. His ability to distract the nation's, and Kansas City's, fans from the latter stages of future Hall of Famer George Brett's career was particularly disturbing, and out of all scale to Jackson's demonstrated ability as a ballplayer. Jackson posted good numbers in 1990—28 home runs, 78 RBIs, and a .272 average—but his status during this period as an international media icon seemed hard to justify in light of Brett's extraordinary accomplishment in winning the batting title in 1990 at the age of thirty-seven!

In 1991, Jackson sustained a hip pointer injury while playing football, and was never the same on the baseball field. The Royals placed him on waivers; later, he made negligible contributions as an occasional DH for the Chicago White Sox.

In summary: Bo didn't know what it was like to play in two leagues in the years before multimillion-dollar contracts and fat endorsement deals. One of the low points of Jackson's much-ballyhooed dual career came shortly after his ill-conceived remarks about his baseball "hobby" in Kansas City. The baseball fans didn't think much of the idea of Jackson's taking the sport so lightly, and certainly the men who preceded him as dual NFL/major-league baseball athletes must have regarded their exploits as anything *but* a hobby. They weren't being paid enough to do otherwise. If either sport had been a hobby, they probably wouldn't have bothered.

MYTH 34

Howard Ehmke Pitched a No-Hitter on September 7, 1923

The ultimate moundsman's mark: Tip of the hat.
But an anti-no-hitter? Who boasts about that?

Sandy Koufax.
Nolan Ryan.
Mike Scott.
Dwight Gooden.
We may remember a lot of things about these great pitchers, but somehow the games people keep coming back to are the no-hitters they threw.

What is it that's so captivating about a no-hitter? They're rare, but so are games in which both teams score fifteen or more runs, and those don't win front-page attention or entries in the *Baseball Encyclopedia*. Perhaps it's the idea of total mastery that accompanies a no-hit, no-run game, the notion that a pitcher, when truly in the "zone," has complete control over the opposing lineup. *That's* something that doesn't happen all too often in baseball (or in life), and it may well be this feature of the no-hitter that secures the most adulation and honor from the baseball world for those who are able to toss one.

If this is the case, the no-hitter attributed to Red Sox pitcher Howard Ehmke in 1923 may be among the least inspiring on the books. How masterful, after all, is a pitcher who no-hits the other team...while allowing a hit?

Be forewarned: This is not a case of a drive that "could have gone either way," but that the official scorer placed in the error column. Such situations have arisen in many no-hitters, and while one can question such calls after the fact, one must also acknowledge that baseball is a game of close calls.

Apparently this one didn't look all that close.

But for a baserunning error by the A's pitcher Slim Harriss, the September 7, 1923, game between Boston and Philadelphia would have gone into the books as just another game, a status some would argue it should hold regardless. Harriss, you see, smashed a double off the right-field wall—but was declared out because he missed touching first base.

Whatever you call what Harriss did, it wasn't the result of Ehmke's bearing down and getting his man out. Real no-hitters don't feature hot drives off of the outfield wall, and this game did.

In the very next game that he pitched, Ehmke was *deprived* of a no-hitter when the official scorer determined that a borderline ground ball was a single, rather than an error. (Again: How many times has *that* deprived someone of a date with history?) Sounds like it was a strange couple of starts for the Red Sox hurler—either he got the no-hitter and he didn't deserve it, or he came within a whisker of earning the no-hitter and he didn't get it.

Those weren't the only fateful contests in which Howard Ehmke took part. He went on to post a total of 20 victories for the Red Sox in 1920; he nearly equaled that mark the following year, with 19 wins. In later years, he never managed to step forward as a starting pitcher in quite the same way...during the regular season. In 1929, having snagged only 7 victories as a starter for Connie Mack's Philadelphia Athletics during the year, Ehmke was named as the surprise starter of the opening game of the World Series against the Cubs. He had scouted the Chicago squad carefully during the final phase of the season, and his homework paid off. He struck out thirteen—at the time, a World Series record—and won, 3–1.

It would have, and probably should have, been a superb career-capper. Ehmke pitched three-plus innings in Game Five, but ran into trouble; he was lifted, but Philadelphia won the game and the series. Had Ehmke retired after the 1929 Series, he would have been the proud owner of a winning lifetime regular-season record. As it happened, he came back to Philadelphia in 1930, went 0–1 for the season, and finished up with an even 166–166 mark.

Woulda, coulda, shoulda...

In summary: Ehmke's "no-no" falls under the "no-yes" category.

MYTH 33

Bucky Dent's Home Run in the 1978 A.L. East Playoff Was the Game's Death Blow to the Boston Red Sox

Dent's hit was the one that carried the day?
Mr. October may have something to say.

Just about every baseball fan can identify Bucky Dent—the light-hitting shortstop whose home run over the Green Monster in the famed division-title playoff game of 1978 saved the day for the Yankees.

Right?

Dent did save the day, didn't he?

Well, sort of. Like Bill Buckner's infamous muffed grounder in the 1986 World Series, Dent's home run (a routine fly ball in any park other than Fenway) was *a* critical moment in the game, but it's not quite accurate to say that it was *the* critical moment in the game. Like Buckner's error, Dent's hit is easily the best *sound-bite* associated with a fateful baseball game. But baseball games are complicated things, and there was a lot more to the Yankees' victory over the Sox on that memorable day.

It was Monday, October 2, 1978. It was time to settle the one-game playoff that would decide the fate of the American League East title that the Sox had seemed to have in hand easily during July. But they had faded, and the Yankees had come on very strong indeed. Near the end of the season, Boston had put on a little kick of its own and tied New York for first place. Now it all came down to one game.

Entering the seventh inning, the Sox were ahead 2–0. Yankees Chris Chambliss and Roy White stroked one-out singles. After another out, the number-nine hitter, Dent, stepped up to face Boston hurler Mike Torrez. Dent fouled the second pitch off his foot, and then, having left the batter's box to walk off the blow, took a new bat from the batboy. Yankee outfielder Mickey Rivers had noticed that the one Dent had been using was cracked. After a few minutes, Dent stepped back in and walloped Torrez's next offering over the left-field fence. Three runs scored. The Yankees led, 3–2.

It was only Dent's fifth home run of 1978.

Yes, Dent's unlikely home run put the Yankees ahead (they added a pad run in the same inning to push the lead to 4–2)...but however unexpected the moment, the game was not yet in the bag. The man who *put* it in the bag—or at any rate gave the Yankees the breathing room they would eventually need—was none other than Reggie Jackson.

Without Jackson's solo eighth-inning home run, which made the score 5–2, the Red Sox could well have reclaimed control of the game. In the home half of the eighth, Jerry Remy doubled, then scored on a Carl Yastrzemski single. Then Carlton Fisk and Fred Lynn singled, leading to another run.

The score: 5–4 Yankees. And that's the way it stayed.

There are any number of other moments from that star-crossed game that are worthy of review—notably Yastrzemski's early homer, and his doomed final at-bat with two outs in the ninth and the tying run only ninety feet away—but the question at hand is whether or not Dent made all the difference, and the fact is that he didn't. In the final analysis it's hard not to conclude that Jackson's home run, which supplied the winning margin, was the most important Yankee hit of the day. Without it, the Red Sox, who came alive in the next inning, might well have sneaked the game into extra innings.

Dent showed off some sparkling play against the Dodgers in the World Series, whom the Yankees beat 4 games to 2 for the second straight year in the Fall Classic. Dent's .417 average, 3 runs scored, and 7 runs batted in earned him the Series MVP award. He played shortstop for the Yankees for the next three seasons, then moved on to Texas and, eventually, Kansas City, where he played his final season in 1984. Dent ended up managing the Yankees for a time in 1989, replacing Dallas Green, who had been fired by George Steinbrenner. Like any number of other Yankee managers of the era, Dent didn't last for long, yielding to Stump Merrill in 1990.

In summary: Dent's wind-driven fly-ball-turned-homer made for a great video—and a great story—but it wasn't the final nail in the Red Sox coffin. That nail was Reggie Jackson's home run in the eighth. (For a similar case of media overkill in a game that dashed the hopes of Red Sox fans, see Myth 39.)

MYTH 32

Alexander Cartwright Was the First Umpire in Organized Baseball

The first-ever umpire to hear an appeal?
Cartwright? That's not what the records reveal.

As discussed elsewhere in this book, much has been attributed to Alexander Cartwright that should not be.

Don't misunderstand. Cartwright should certainly be regarded as *one of* the important figures in the genesis of the game, and so should many of his friends on the Knickerbocker Base Ball Club. That having been said, it must also be said that Alexander Cartwright has all too often been given responsibility for single-handedly transforming (or even inventing) the game of baseball. In fact he has been nearly canonized in a way that would certainly have surprised him and the amateur athletes with whom he seems to have passed pleasant, invigorating days on the ballfield. The New York bank teller has, in later years, been pressed into service as a kind of god in the skies above the firmament of the national pastime: the bearded Creator of the game Americans know and love.

Among the "guiding hand" myths promulgated about Cartwright is the notion that he served as umpire for the celebrated game played between the Knickerbockers and the New York Club on June 19, 1846. Did he?

Leaving aside for the moment the fateful question of whether or not this game represents the first organized baseball contest—a thorny issue that's likely to yield more than a few surprises—let's look at a few simple facts about the contest of June 19. (For a fuller discussion of the complicated question of the status of that game as "the first baseball game in history," see Myth 4.)

- The scoresheets in the Knickerbocker game book feature space for the name of the umpire.
- Many (but not all) matches recorded in this book feature the signature of the presiding umpire.
- Cartwright's name does not appear in the umpire's slot for the June 19, 1846, game.

Is it *possible* Cartwright served as umpire in this game? Yes. Is there any *evidence* he did so? Not a shred. But his posthumous status as Beneficent Sportsman and Creator of the National Game seems to have led many to argue that, whether or not Cartwright pulled umpiring duties for this contest, he certainly *should* have.

But focusing on the (unknown) umpire for the June 19 game is actually irrelevant. The question ought to be, Who is first *recorded* as having officiated a game involving the Knickerbockers? The answer is William R. Wheaton, one of the founding members of the club. He stepped aside as a player and, as his signature attests, served as umpire in a game that took place during *the year before* the supposed "first game." Wheaton did the job on October 6, 1845.

Cartwright was *an* umpire for many of the early Knickerbocker games, but he was not the first to record his name on a scoresheet. For that, we must recognize Wheaton, a young New York lawyer who had been, in the previous month, one of the two Knickerbocker officials to have affixed his signature to the club rules approved on September 23, 1845. (The other was William Tucker; both men were part of a larger by-laws committee.)

Interesting side note: Given his known (underline *known*) role as an umpire and rule-writer, there appears to be more basis for assigning Wheaton a greater measure of credit for formalizing and implementing the rules of the Knicker-bocker Base Ball Club than Cartwright. Yet it is Cartwright, not Wheaton, who holds a place of honor in the Baseball Hall of Fame. Perhaps both men—and perhaps others— should be accorded a measure of the glory that has been Cartwright's as a result of his association with the Knicker-bocker Base Ball Club. Whether or not Wheaton deserves a place in the Hall, however, it is important to remember that the Knickerbocker club *was* a club, not a vehicle for a single person to dominate. It was a *social* entity first and foremost, and one that was not always given, in its early years, to observing the rules it set down for itself, umpires or no umpires.

Wheaton was one of three umpires to oversee another important game that preceded the June 19, 1846, contest, the October 25, 1845, match between New York and Brooklyn that inspired what is now believed to be the first newspaper report of a baseball game. (See Myth 30.)

In summary: No close call here. Alexander Cartwright was *one* of baseball's first umpires, but there is documentary evidence that points to William R. Wheaton as the first to sign on in this capacity. Wheaton did so at a time when the basic principles of the game we know as baseball were still in an early state of their development, but the fact remains that he is known to have officiated a game before Cartwright is known to have done so. (See also Myth 4.)

MYTH 31

Hall of Famer Roger Bresnahan Invented Shin Guards in 1907

What ended the pain of a home plate collision?
Bresnahan's tools? A faulty decision.

Feel like enduring a collision at the plate? How about an errant pitch or a foul tip? Big-league catchers have always been on the receiving end of all of these. In the early days of the game, though, they dealt with such physical perils without the benefit of modern safety equipment. Not surprisingly, a lot of them got pretty badly banged up.

Catcher Roger Bresnahan is in the Hall of Fame, thanks in part to his work developing baseball safety equipment. Bresnahan's research was well motivated; he was out to find ways to keep from getting hurt. He experimented with a batting helmet in 1905 after being hit in the head with a ball. Unfortunately his innovation was not adopted by players at the big-league level; if it had been, the tragic death of Cleveland shortstop Ray Chapman might have been avoided. (For a full discussion of the incident, see Myth 8.) In 1907, Bresnahan started wearing shin guards, presumably the result of some unpleasant experiences behind the plate as a catcher. There were snickers at first, but eventually other big-league catchers followed Bresnahan's example.

Bresnahan helped to make shin guards standard equipment in organized baseball. But was he the first to use them?

In 1905, the same year Bresnahan was tinkering with the idea of a helmet that might protect a batter from needless exposure to severe head injury, a rookie catcher by the name of Jay Justin "Nig" Clarke joined the Cleveland team. Two years before Bresnahan's shin guard experiment, Clarke was wearing soccer guards under his socks.

Clarke, a solid but raw-armed defensive catcher who hailed from Canada, spent nine years in the big leagues and compiled a .254 lifetime average. Although he once earned a measure of notoriety for allowing Germany Schaefer to steal second, then first, then second again (Schaefer was trying to draw a throw so a runner on third could score), Clarke's workmanlike career did not earn him much in the way of popular adulation. He didn't land in the Hall of Fame. Maybe he shouldn't have, but he should at least be recognized for coming up with a darned good idea. Although Bresnahan, who also improved the design of the catcher's mask, seems to have done more to *popularize* shin guards, there's reason to believe the credit for the initial use of this equipment in a baseball setting should have gone to Clarke.

Bresnahan posted a lifetime .279 batting average. In 1905 (the same year Clarke began to play around with shin protection equipment) Bresnahan caught every game in the 1905 World Series. His team, the Giants, won the Series handily, thanks in part to Bresnahan's .313 Series average. In later years he served as a player-manager for the Cardinals and Cubs (posting a career .432 winning percentage) and as a coach for the Giants and Tigers.

In summary: Ask a catcher whether it's a big deal to have a little more protection than a pants leg against a set of flying cleats attached to a speeding baserunner. Bresnahan—and Clarke before him—knew it was. Only one of them should be recognized as the first to use shinguards, and the vote on this end goes to Clarke.

MYTH 30

The First Newspaper Story About Baseball Appeared in 1853

A late-breaking story, perhaps, but it's true:
The topic that year was far from brand-new.

These days, newspapers are crammed with baseball news: statistics, photos, summaries, schedules. There are even newspapers whose sole aim is to report on breaking baseball news. But in the very earliest days of the game, the period when the first attempts were made to formalize the game's rules, America's oldest media format carried precious little in the way of reports about the pursuit that would become the National Pastime.

Many sources have held that the first newspaper stories concerning baseball did not appear until 1853, when the *New York Mercury* ran two stories—one on May 1 that featured a general mention of the sport, and another on July 10 that offered an account of a recent game. It turns out, however, that printed baseball news goes back a few years earlier.

In a 1980 article appearing in the *Journal of Sport History*, Melvin Adelman reported that the *New York Herald* had run a story in its October 21, 1845, issue about a forthcoming game to be played between the New York Club and the Brooklyn

Club. This story is now thought to be the earliest newspaper mention of the game of baseball.

Ten years later, Edward L. Widmer reported that the *New York Morning News* had run, on October 22, 1845, an account of the very same New York/Brooklyn game *after* it had been played, complete with box score. This story in the *Morning News* now stands as the first-ever postgame account of a baseball contest.

Future scholarship may unearth more facts in this area. In any event, the 1853 date does not reflect the first newspaper reporting of the game of baseball.

It's worth noting that the *Morning News* story refers to the contest on which it was reporting as an instance of "the time-honored game of Base," and not as some newfangled way of passing the time. Here, as in so many chapters of the game's very early history, the search for "firsts" and "origins" is beset with difficulties and stubbornly uncooperative facts. The strike of 1994 notwithstanding, baseball may well be best regarded as a "neverending" and "neverbeginning" story, a phenomenon that changes slowly but perceptibly throughout its history, and that extends, in some form, into both the past and the future as far as we may care to trace it. As such, it's a pretty good representative for all sorts of supposedly common experiences that turn out to reflect (hold the phone) transcendent realities of one kind or another—like first love, say, or the creative process, or a piece of great folk music that's been handed down for uncounted, and probably uncountable, generations. These things, too, sometimes seem never to have "started" in any meaningful sense of the word, and their derivations are open-ended in a strangely exhilarating way.

Maybe that's why so many of us get reverent looks in our eyes when we talk about the National Pastime, and treat visits to ballparks as though they were trips to cathedrals. It never really started. With any luck, it will never really end.

In summary: In our present state of knowledge, the "scoop" associated with first mentioning the game of baseball must be awarded to the *Herald* of October 21, 1845. The credit for the first box score belongs to the October 22, 1845, *Morning News.*

MYTH 29

Duane Kuiper (Cleveland Indians and San Francisco Giants, 1974–1985) Was the Worst Nonpitching Home-Run Hitter of All Time

The question is, who had the least home-run power?
The Indians' Kuiper had numbers that tower.

How low is low?

Not long after his retirement as an active player in 1985, second baseman Duane Kuiper, who'd played with the Indians in the American League and the Giants in the National League, was credited with a dubious honor. Kuiper, who had come to bat a total of 3,379 times, had a lifetime home-run total of (drum roll, please) one.

The lone blast, which came in 1977 off White Sox pitcher Steve Stone, was thought to have earned Kuiper the distinction (such as it is) of being the worst position player of all time when it comes to home-run production. This is not to say that Kuiper was a poor *hitter*. He retired with a more-than-respectable .271 batting average, and was thrice the only man in the lineup to get a hit during a game. (He pulled the spoiler act against pitchers Andy Hassler, Nolan Ryan, and Ron Guidry.) He was also a superior fielder who twice led American League second basemen in fielding percentage.

But he was no slugger.

Assuming a minimum number of career at-bats of 2,000—a step that eliminates most pitchers from consideration—Kuiper's career home-run percentage shows up at an infinitesimal .00029. That's pretty slim, and apparently Kuiper liked it that way. (As Kuiper put it, "One is better than none, but any more than that and people start expecting them.")

But it turns out that Kuiper *can't* lay claim to the title of worst-ever launcher of four-baggers. The all-time record for home-run ineptitude among players with 2,000 or more at-bats belongs not to the Cleveland and San Francisco second baseman, but to Bill Holbert, a catcher and outfielder who played twelve years in the National League and American Association between 1876 and 1888. Holbert posted a lifetime batting average of .208 (far below Kuiper's), and seems to have passed a relatively undistinguished major-league career with five different teams. According to the renowned statistical wizards with the wit, energy, and perseverance necessary to calculate these sorts of things, Holbert's status as a baseball immortal emerges when his lifetime home-run percentage is ranked against the rest of the men who've logged time in the major leagues.

Among players with at least 2,000 career at-bats, Holbert beats out even Duane Kuiper as the least distinguished power hitter ever. In 2,335 at-bats, Holbert failed to hit a single home run.

That's "zero," with a z. The resulting home-run percentage, if you're keeping score at home, looks like this: .00000. It's the kind of record that may be tied someday, but it will never be broken.

So unless someone comes up with evidence that indicates Kuiper failed to touch a base during his single, glorious home-run trot, he is off the hook, and Holbert heads the list of baseball's ultimate antipower hitters.

In summary: Catcher-outfielder Bill Holbert is the record holder. Kuiper—who has claimed that he *tried* not to launch any round-trippers after his 1977 shot against Steve Stone— is in little danger of being mistaken for Jimmie Foxx in the home-run department, but at least he's on the board.

MYTH 28

Night Baseball First Appeared in the Mid-to-Late Thirties

A night game is one of today's cherished sights,
But it raises a question: Who turned on the lights?

How long can a good idea go unimplemented? Quite a while, apparently. Take night baseball.

A good many people believe that big-league night baseball began in 1938, on the night of June 15. Although this certainly was a landmark night in baseball history—Johnny Vander Meer of the Reds, facing the Brooklyn Dodgers at home, pitched his second consecutive no-hitter that night—this date marks the first night game ever played *at Ebbetts Field*. The first night game ever played in the major leagues took place three years earlier, on May 24, 1935, at Crosley Field in Cincinnati. (In case you were wondering about the outcome, the Reds beat the Phillies 2–1.) Before that game, Franklin Roosevelt pushed a button in the White House, thereby inaugurating the era of baseball under the lights in faraway Cincinnati.

But how "new" was the idea of night baseball? Not all that new, it turns out.

In fact, the first night game of any kind had been played nearly fifty-five years before the 1935 game in Crosley Field. Shortly after the invention of the incandescent light, two

Boston department store teams played a night game near Hull, Massachusetts, to prove the utility of the newfangled invention. Other experiments followed.

Night baseball had proven its ability to draw a crowd a quarter of a century before FDR pushed the button that illuminated Crosley Field. In 1910, George Cahill showed off a lighting system to Chicago owner Charles Comiskey, but he made no headway with the White Sox owner, despite the presence of 20,000 fans at an exhibition game played by two amateur teams under a set of portable lights at Comiskey Park.

Showing a remarkable lack of foresight, big-league owners refused to see the potential of Cahill's innovation. Yankee boss Ed Barrow had his doubts about the whole idea, and he wearily dismissed the notion of night baseball as "a passing attraction."

History proved Cahill right and Barrow wrong, but it sure took a while for night baseball to reach the big leagues. It is worth noting, however, that the the Cincinnati Reds were *not* the first professional team to install lights. That honor goes to the Independence, Kansas, team of the Class C Western Association, who set up their system in 1930.

Pittsburgh's Forbes Field served as the setting for yet *another* memorable pre-1935 night game when two legendary teams from the Negro Leagues teams, the Kansas City Monarchs and the hometown Homestead Grays, played there on the night of July 25, 1930. This was a pivotal game in the history of the Negro Leagues; the Grays' catcher walked out because the Monarchs' lighting system didn't meet his standards, and manager Judy Johnson was forced to pick a promising local player from the stands to fill the position. The player's name: Josh Gibson, acknowledged by many to be the greatest home-run hitter of all time, black or white.

Even decades after the triumph of night baseball (nowadays, it's even been played at Wrigley Field), purists have argued that there are *some* situations where night games simply don't belong, and at times it's hard to deny that they have a point. The inaugural World Series night game, which took place in 1971, was the first of a seemingly endless series of scheduling concessions to network television executives eager to milk the last possible ratings point from the Fall Classic. It was, as so many of these games still are, a chilly affair. Commissioner Bowie Kuhn, apparently conscious that the cameras were on him, remained hatless and refused to put on an overcoat throughout the game, lest anyone capture an image of him acknowledging the same grim meteorological reality faced by tens of thousands of fans in the same stadium. Cold weather or no, daytime World Series games have since gone the way of the dinosaur, a development that has had a pronounced "chilling effect" not only on fans lucky enough to get tickets, but also on television viewers (kids, for instance) who can't stay up late enough to watch the contests. That's the way to build long-term interest in the game, all right.

In summary: Night baseball was an emerging phenomenon that probably should have made it to the big leagues a good deal earlier than it did. Its roots go back to the nineteenth century, and if it bore the hallmarks of a passing fad in the very earliest artificially lit games, the considerable crowd that showed up for the 1910 game at Comiskey certainly should be recognized as evidence of the idea's early popularity and potential.

MYTH 27

Aaron Stern Initiated the First Ladies' Day in 1886

With women attending, the game changed around,
But Stern wasn't the person who first tracked them down.

Women—in attendance at baseball games? There was a time when the very notion was revolutionary. But that time was some years before 1886, when some sources claim the first Ladies' Day was observed at a ballpark.

Although he has been credited with developing the marketing maneuver known as Ladies' Day, nineteenth-century Cincinnati owner Aaron Stern seems only to have been putting into practice an idea that had been around for some years. Like any number of supposed "breakthrough" promotional ideas, this one seems to have been adapted from someone else.

Initially the idea seems to have been to change the deportment of the fans at the game as much as it was to draw new fans to the ballyards. Baseball fans in the dawning years of the game were a pretty rough crowd. As Henry Chadwick wrote in baseball's very early days:

> We have avowed ourselves on all occasions the open foe to all those evil influences which . . . have only too surely crept in as a drawback to the permanent establishment of

the game as a pastime thoroughly unobjectionable....
We claim to rank among our enemies every low-minded
vicious "rough," whether clad in broad-cloth or
homespun; every professional gambler who aims to
make rival clubs his tools, and every foul-mouthed,
blaspheming "sport," whose only idea of enjoyment,
connected with any game or trial or skill, consists of the
amount of animal gratification it can afford him, either
as a means of gambling, of various excitement, or of
intemperance. Our ambition, beyond that of
endeavoring to establish a national game for all
Americans, has been to earn the respect and esteem only
of the best classes of the ball-playing fraternity.

Despite Chadwick's fulminations, corruption, drunkenness,
and chaos marred many a baseball game in the years
following the Civil War. Promoters believed that the presence of women at the games might add a sense of cultivation
to the proceedings, and cut down on the ungentlemanly
behavior (and particularly the excessive indulgence in con-
sumption of alcoholic beverages) that so often served as a
sore distraction during the games.

The original Ladies' Days began as early as 1876, when
one team decided to set aside the last Thursday of the month
as a day when men could bring female acquaintances and
family members to the ball field. The days became quite
popular in the next decade. Brooklyn, as well as a number of
other teams, eventually began stuffing its playing calendars
with Ladies' Days. Like many things about baseball to
which fans respond enthusiastically, the practice seems to
have become something of an instant tradition, if that's not
too much of a contradiction in terms.

Although he can't be credited with having been the first
to stage a Ladies' Day, Cincinnati's Aaron Stern may well
have been one of the most astute practitioners of the

technique for drawing in fans. Apparently Stern noticed that there were considerably more women than usual in the stands when his good-looking pitcher Tony Mullane (nick-named "the Apollo of the Box") took the mound. Stern started playing Mullane against the weaker teams his men faced—the ones least likely to draw a big crowd—and began billing Mullane's starts as Ladies' Days.

Tony Mullane, by the way, was remarkable for a lot more than his good looks. He was an early rabble-rouser on behalf of a ballplayer's right to be paid what he was worth, and a man who put his money where his mouth was. Mullane was suspended for the entire 1885 season because he wouldn't acknowledge his sale to a team for which he didn't want to play; he also refused to play for part of the 1892 season when the National League instituted pay cuts. First and foremost, he was, by all accounts, a truly extraordinary athlete. Mullane was the first ambidextrous pitcher in the history of the game, a fact he used to strategic advantage. Because Mullane played without a glove, and often did not decide until the last minute which hand he would use to pitch, batters had no idea which direction the pitch would be coming from! He was a switch hitter who posted a serviceable .243 average, and he played every position except catcher. But it was as a pitcher that he earned his greatest renown. Mullane went 35–15 in 1883, led his league in shutouts twice, and completed a remarkable 469 games over the course of his career. As we might say today, the guy could do it all. No wonder he drew enthusiastic fans of both genders.

In summary: Who first came up with the idea? It's hard to say, but the practice of setting aside a special day to welcome female fans to the ballpark is known to have been adopted years before Aaron Stern began capitalizing on Tony Mullane's good looks and extraordinary skills.

MYTH 26

The System of Hand Signals to Signify Balls and Strikes Was the Idea of Umpire Cy Rigler, Who Wanted to Help Out Deaf Outfielder William Hoy

Sometimes an idea works, sometimes it doesn't.
Who started signals? Well, we know who it wasn't.

This is one that probably *ought* to have happened, but didn't.

The story goes that William Ellsworthy "Dummy" Hoy, who was deaf, managed to convince umpire Cy Rigler to use his right hand to signal strike decisions. When Rigler agreed to do so, we are told, Hoy was not only able to keep track of the umpire's calls while at bat, but also had an easier time determining how things stood at the plate while playing defense in the outfield.

Makes sense, right? The story certainly seems to contain enough plausible elements to be legitimate, and it definitely has caught on over the years.

Rigler *was* an umpire during the period in question. Apparently, he *did* use a system of hand signals while umpiring in Indiana before he made it to the major leagues.

Hoy *was* a standout player who could not, in fact, hear (see Myth 15); he batted .288 over the course of a fourteen-year career and stole 597 bases. Hoy led the league in walks in 1891 and 1901, and in at-bats in 1899. He had his best year at the plate with Cincinnati in 1894, posting a .312 season average. He was one of the most accomplished fielders of his day: on June 19, 1889, Hoy secured his place among an elite group of outfielders by throwing out three runners at the plate in a single game. Because of his physical handicap, Hoy went by the inelegant nickname "Dummy" during his decade and a half in the big leagues, and he played with seven different teams. (He was one of a very few players— twenty-nine in all—to have played in *four* different major leagues: the National League, the Players' League, the American Association, and the American League.)

It may seem to make sense to attribute the modern system of arm and hand signals to Hoy's input—and it probably would have made things a little easier for the guy— but there's no way he deserves the credit.

Hoy retired from the game in 1902, after stroking a cool .290 in 70 games for Cincinnati. Rigler, who *is* credited with originating the raising-the-arm routine behind the plate, thereby relieving the umpire of the responsibility to be heard throughout the ballpark, first used the system in the big leagues 1905. Some believe a system of hand signals among umpires was in place before Rigler arrived in the majors; others don't. However you slice it, Rigler couldn't have developed the system in response to Hoy's handicap.

While the legend of Rigler's innovation springing out of Hoy's request makes a good story, it doesn't fit in with the facts.

In summary: Rigler should be credited with the innovation on his own, and in 1905, when he first gave it a try in the big leagues. Hoy's career should be recognized as all the more remarkable, because it was probably conducted for extended periods with less than complete information about exactly what was going on at the plate.

MYTH 25

Babe Ruth Benefited From a Home-Field Advantage at the "House That Ruth Built" During His Historic 1927 Season

The park he made famous was clearly red-hot,
The year Babe bashed all those round-trippers? (Not.)

You might *think* that Babe Ruth would have hit more home runs at home than on the road during the year he hit a superhuman 60 home runs (and a lot of people do), but you'd be wrong.

The so-called House That Ruth Built—Yankee Stadium—was not the launching pad for most of the Bambino's home runs during his storied 1927 season. The Babe hit 32 of his record 60 home runs on the road that year.

That's just one of the surprising statistics associated with Ruth's performance in 1927.

Wherever and however he hit during that landmark year, Ruth put up some truly staggering numbers as a member of the team that many regard as the greatest of all time. In addition to besting teammate Lou Gehrig for the home-run title (the second-place Gehrig launched a paltry 47 round-trippers), Ruth led the league in slugging percentage (.772), bases on balls (138), and runs scored (158).

Yet surprisingly, the Babe's mammoth year at the plate

did not bring him the RBI crown. The American League leader in that category was Ruth's teammate Lou Gehrig, who checked in with 175. (Gehrig led the league in doubles, with 52, which didn't hurt.) The Iron Horse also bested Ruth in the batting-average department, .373 to .356, but neither man came within twenty points of Harry Heillmann, who, at .398, was the league's top hitter—at least as far as average is concerned. When it came to total hits, neither Ruth nor Gehrig came in first. That honor went to their teammate Earle Combs.

Suffice it to say that, while there are some unexpected statistics associated with Ruth's extraordinary 1927 year at the plate, his season was nevertheless a landmark one in baseball history. More would follow. It seems appropriate to note here that there is still a good deal of controversy surrounding one of the most widely circulated remarks ever attributed to Ruth about his own playing record. The story goes that someone once told Ruth that the $80,000 salary he received for playing for the Yankees was $5,000 more than that which President Herbert Hoover received for leading the nation. Supposedly, the Bambino simply shrugged and said, "I had a better year than he did." The anecdote makes a great quote—and it perfectly captures a time when the nation *needed* a hero of Ruth's dimensions—but legendary sportswriter Red Smith had his doubts that the Babe would have responded so quickly with the wisecrack. "He was just too uninformed about politics," Smith opined. Some experts consider the remark to be the creation of Depression-era newspaper writers. Others swear Ruth made the joke himself. This one may never be resolved.

In summary: Ruth hit "only" 28 home runs at home during the fabled 1927 season, a surprising stat that is one of several associated with his performance that year.

MYTH 24

Pitchers Don't Win Batting Titles

Some pitchers can hit, and the stat may intrigue,
But who wudda thunk one could beat a whole league?

Very few big-league pitchers have distinguished themselves at the plate. Sure, every once in a while you run into an all-around athlete who manages to make a splash on the mound and in the batter's box—Babe Ruth, who set an all-time .304 lifetime hitting mark as a pitcher, comes to mind, as does Brooklyn Dodger ace and occasional pinch-hitter Don Newcombe, who hit .359 in 117 at-bats in 1955. For the most part, however, the pitcher's reputation as an "automatic out" is justly earned. (See Myth 47 concerning the origin of the designated-hitter rule.)

And even that rare pitcher who is able to crack the occasional base hit certainly *wouldn't* be able to amass the necessary at-bats to win a batting title, right?

Well, that statement holds true for the two major leagues with which we are most familiar—the American and National leagues—but for the American Association, the big-league rival to the N.L. in the 1880s and early 1890s, there was one standout player who, in one season, appeared in more games as a pitcher than he did at any other position... and posted the top batting average in the league.

He was Guy Hecker, a Louisville star who bore the

intriguing nickname "Blond Guy," and who posted a .342 average for Louisville in 1886, thereby becoming the only pitcher in history to win a big-league batting crown, something not even Babe Ruth would do. Hecker beat out teammate Pete Browning, who played center field, by only two points! Hecker won 27 games that year, and also played a number of games at first base and in the outfield for Louisville. One suspects the team was eager to find a way to keep his bat in the lineup; that he was able to perform so well as both an everyday player and a pitcher is nothing short of extraordinary. For the sake of comparison, see the statistics Babe Ruth posted in his "transitional" 1919 season (Myth 12).

Hecker's often-overlooked feat is only one of several high points in a remarkably strong career; he threw a no-hitter as a rookie, hit three home runs in a game, and crossed the plate seven times in another. In that game, he went 6-for-7 at the plate with three (inside-the-park) home runs! Not bad for a pitcher.

Despite sterling contributions from both Hecker and Browning, the Colonels were an average team at best that finished well out of the money in 1886. They won 66 and lost 70, finishing twenty-five and a half games behind league-leading St. Louis. Three years later, with Hecker (5–11, 5.59 ERA) and Browning (.256, only 32 RBIs) still in the lineup, they would compile a 27–111 record that would put them in the running for the title of worst team in the history of major league baseball (see Myth 50).

How does that Joni Mitchell song go—the one about not knowing what you've got till it's gone?

In summary: Guy Hecker was the exception to the (usually reliable) notion that pitchers are not to be confused with the strongest hitters in the league. His accomplishment may well never be repeated in the big leagues.

MYTH 23

The New York Yankees Established the Greatest Dominance Over Their Competition in the History of Organized Baseball

Mirror, mirror, on the wall—
Which team stomped rivals the hardest of all?

Yankees. Dynasty. Baseball. The three words just seem to flow into one another, don't they?

As well they should. It's impossible to dispute that, over the long haul, the Yankees represent the most successful team in baseball history at any level. Between 1921 and 1964, the team won twenty-nine pennants.

But that's over the long haul. The Yankees didn't win the pennant *every* year, although sometimes it seemed like it (especially if you were a Boston Red Sox fan in the late forties). Their dynasty was marked by some comparatively brief, but from their opponents' point of view gratifying, downturns in team fortune. The Philadelphia A's emerged as the team to beat in the American League between 1929 and 1931; Detroit snagged pennants in 1934, 1935, and 1940; the Red Sox took the flag in 1946; and Cleveland fans like to point out that it is the 1954 Indians, and not a Yankee squad, that holds the mark for most total victories in a season, with 111.

It's probably most accurate to say that the justly praised, long-running Yankee dynasty is actually a series of *smaller* dynasties, strung together over a four-decade span of time, with occasional second-place finishes thrown in by the Almighty to keep the rest of the league from losing hope completely. (As for fans of the National League Brooklyn Dodgers, who typically faced, and lost to, the Yankees in World Series of the latter part of this era, the Supreme Being seems to have singled them out for similar punishment, but, in keeping with the general pattern established in the American League, granted them a single memorable year of triumph—1955—without altering the grand scheme of things.)

In other words, as awesome as they were, the Yankees never *completely* dominated a six-or-seven-year stretch of time in their league. But no team can win *every* pennant during such a protracted period, right?

Well, one squad did.

There was a professional team that put together a string of seasons that surpassed even the Yankees' reign at the top of the heap. The team was the Baltimore Orioles of the International League, which won seven, count 'em, seven pennants between the years 1919 and 1925.

That's right, they didn't finish a single year out of first place.

The Orioles of this period and this league—not to be confused with the contemporary Baltimore Orioles, who are descended from the St. Louis Browns, or the National League Baltimore Orioles, who became part of the senior circuit in 1892 and emerged as a league powerhouse in 1894—may have gone into the books as a minor-league team, but they were generally regarded as superior to the majority of the big-league squads of the day. As if to

··

underline the point, a good chunk of the core players from the Oriole glory years eventually found their way to Philadelphia, where they enjoyed a period of American League dominance with Connie Mack's Athletics. (Does the name Lefty Grove ring a bell?)

There has never been a professional baseball team that dominated its circuit as the Orioles did the International League, and that includes the New York Yankees. There may never be another one. Baltimore won the flag in 1920 by twenty-six and a half games. You read correctly; the *second-place* team finished twenty-six and a half off the pace. The next year, the Orioles won 27 games in a row, en route to a 119-victory season. (The I.L. season ran 168 games that year.)

Why were the Orioles so good? They were that rarity among minor-league teams, an organization that refused to let go of its players for less than they were worth. (Perhaps the organization was stung by the experience of having recently sold a very, very young Babe Ruth to the Boston Red Sox.) Jack Dunn, owner and manager of the Orioles, developed a way of hanging on to good talent unless he got an offer that suited him. He usually didn't.

In summary: The Yankees may be untouchable when the subject is long-term dominance of a league, but when it comes to identifying a particular *team nucleus* that came out on top year in and year out, the Orioles rank number one in the history of organized baseball. Given today's minor-league system and an economic environment that makes it more difficult to retain the same core team at the big-league level for very long, it seems unlikely that another squad will challenge the Orioles' dominance in this area anytime soon.

MYTH 22

Chicago Outfielder Bill Lange Crashed Through a Fence to Make a Spectacular Grab of a Fly Ball

Not even the wall could make Lange stop—
Or so it was told. The tale's over the top.

For years, baseball fans were told—and then spread—the tale of how Chicago Colts outfielder Bill Lange made a spectacular, through-the-wall catch of a screaming fly ball "sometime back in the 1890s." Did it really happen?

In the 1890s, Lange was one of the most exciting National League hitters, and a standout defensive player. He was known both for his tremendous running ability and his propensity for showy catches. A. H. Spink, who founded The *Sporting News*, called him "Ty Cobb enlarged, fully as great in speed, batting skill, and base running." His best years came in 1895, when he set a club record that still stands by hitting .389, and in 1897, when he hit .340 and stole 73 bases. Although the batting marks didn't even get him into the National League's top five in either season, Lange's stolen-base total led the league in 1897.

How did the story about his crashing through a fence get started? For a long time, no one was sure. In later years there were many versions of the story, but they usually had some common elements. Supposedly Chicago was playing Washington, and was leading 6–5 when Washinton's Kip Selbach drove a ball deep into center field. Lange, apparently en route to another of his trademark showoff catches, was said to have dived for the ball, somersaulted, then careened *right through* the outfield wall. When he returned to the field of play, the story went, he was clutching the ball. Chicago carried the day.

Sounds great. But when, exactly, did it happen?

Researcher Arthur Ahrens of the Society for American Baseball Research wondered that, too. He combed through newspapers and never found any mention of the spectacular catch that sent the Chicago outfielder through the wall. What he *did* find was a report of a game that almost certainly gave rise to the Lange myth. It had all the elements of the story that had been passed down for decades—the broken fence, the great catch, the Chicago victory—but it had them in a slightly different order.

Chicago *was* playing Washington during the game in question. The date was August 31, 1896, and the game was scoreless after ten innings. Chicago first baseman George Decker was hit by a pitch that broke his arm. Washington's Kip Selbach—he's the fellow who was supposed to have hit the drive that Lange caught by means of eating a mouthful of fence—put a hole in an outfield wall with the end of a ladder so that Decker could be taken directly to the hospital. When the game got back under way, Bill Lange *did* make a spectacular grab in right, but he didn't go through a fence in the process. The game went into the eleventh inning. *Washington* won the game, not Chicago.

Other than those few discrepancies, though, the oft-told story of Lange's fence-busting grab was right on target.

Lange left the game for good after the 1899 season to get married, apparently less than thrilled about the strain that a ballplayer's life would put on his relationship with his wife.

(Unfortunately, the marriage ultimately ended in divorce.) His career went into the books with a sparkling .330 lifetime hitting average and 399 stolen bases.

In summary: Lange was apparently a great deal of fun to watch in the outfield, and he was probably one of the most dynamic players of his era. The truth of the matter, though, is that he never made the famous through-the-wall catch for which he received credit for so many years.

MYTH 21

Babe Ruth Hit 714 Home Runs (As We'd Reckon Them)

That seven-fourteen mark is sure hard to figure;
If we'd been counting, the number'd be bigger.

Okay, okay, this one's a quibble that people could argue either way. But it's a fascinating quibble nonetheless.

For many years the most celebrated record in all of baseball, Babe Ruth's lifetime home-run total nevertheless deserves a note of explanation. (I was going to propose that it deserved an asterisk, but then we've probably had more than enough when it comes to asterisks in the category of home-run totals.)

Although Ruth hit 714 home runs during his storied career *according to the rules of the day*, this total does not reflect a blast of the Babe's that would have gone into his yearly numbers if he'd been playing under today's regulations. Confused? Read on.

In 1918, Ruth hit what we would call a game-winning home run that went into the books as a triple. Why? Under the prevailing method of scoring, a winning run scored by the home team in its last at-bat always *ended the game*, no matter what type of hit brought that run about. Because the Bambino's hit came about with a man on first base while the score was tied, the system credited him not with a four-base hit, but with a three-base hit.

Seems kind of unfair to the batter, doesn't it? Well, evidently that's what the people who tinker with the rules thought, too. Before long baseball duly scored *all* the runs that come about on a game-winning hit, and credited the batters accordingly with the hits they had coming to them as a result of the play's coming to its natural conclusion. As it happened, Ruth—still spending something like half his time as a pitcher, mind you—tied for the 1918 league lead in home runs with Tilly Walker of the Athletics, who had nearly a hundred more at-bats. The next year, Ruth stroked 29 homers for the Red Sox, easily besting Walker. And this in a year in which Ruth missed a good chunk of the season! (For a discussion of that controversial absence, see Myth 18. For a detailed review of some surprising home-run totals during the dead-ball era, see Myth 36. For a look at the fascinating transition Ruth made from superb starting pitcher to everyday slugger—and what was responsible for that transition—see Myth 12.)

Now, then. Does this story about Ruth mean that the rules that held at the time of a game's completion shouldn't govern the statistics connected to it? Does it mean that every home-run total from before the rules were changed in this regard should be reevaluated? Does it mean that Henry Aaron *didn't* break Ruth's home run record when we all thought he did, but instead broke the record when he hit his 716th home-run?

Naah. But when you're dealing with a player of Ruth's stature, it's interesting to take a look at all the angles. Since this is the only time Ruth can be said to have fallen into the peculiar statistical glitch of having been robbed of a (contemporary) home run, it's probably worth knowing about when considering his overall accomplishments.

Ruth also walked a guy during a perfect game that his

team won, and if *that's* not a statistical glitch of some kind, I don't know what is. In 1917, the Babe was ejected for arguing a call with the umpire after issuing the fourth ball to the game's first batter; Boston reliever Ernie Shore came in and retired all twenty-seven of the Washington Senators who came to bat that day. The runner was caught stealing.

Ruth is also the only player in the history of major-league baseball who ended a World Series by being thrown out on an attempted stolen base. It happened during the seventh game of the 1926 Series against the St. Louis Cardinals; there were two outs in the ninth, and the Babe represented the tying run. Wouldn't you have loved to be a fly on the locker room wall afterward?

Let's face it. Weird things had a way of happening around the guy. (See Myth 1.)

In summary: This one's a little bizarre, and it certainly falls into the "can of worms" category in that any attempt to argue for a total of 715 for Ruth opens a bewildering array of scoring and procedural doors that probably should remain closed for the greater good of the game. But from a certain point of view, one might, in a rash, unguarded moment, be permitted to wonder—privately, in the dead of night, with all the blinds drawn, and after having promised not to come to any conclusions on the matter—whether the Babe's home-run total for 1918 could have been reckoned as 12, rather than 11.

MYTH 20

Ty Cobb Was No Home-Run Hitter

Could Cobb hit home runs? It's hard to conceive it,
But the numbers don't lie, so we'd better believe it.

Take a good, long look at the following list. Which man doesn't belong?

> Babe Ruth
> Ted Williams
> Mickey Mantle
> George Foster
> Ty Cobb
> Stan Musial
> Reggie Jackson

All right, time's up. What's your answer?

As you may have guessed by now, it's a trick question. But weren't you at least *tempted* to respond "Ty Cobb"?

The correct answer is Stan Musial.

Why? Because every other man on the list—including Ty Cobb—led the major leagues in home runs at least once in his career.

The steady Musial not only never led the major leagues in home runs—he never led the *National* League in home runs. Then again, he had some pretty stiff competition, and he did hit a total of 475 homers over the course of his career. But back to Cobb.

Most of us have an image of Ty Cobb as something other than a hitter of round-trippers. Yet the king of the dead-ball era did in fact lead the big leagues in home-run production one season. The year in question was 1909. The Georgia Peach blasted a total of nine, count 'em, nine round-trippers that year.

Hey, it was more than anyone else hit, right?

In case you were wondering, the Sociopathic One hit a total of 118 home runs over the course of his career. Even acknowledging that he played a good many years, and that a number of these homers were inside-the-park jobs, that's still a pretty respectable total for his period—and it's more than such lively-ball era players as George Sisler, Frankie Crosetti, Monte Irvin, and Wes Westrum managed to hit during *their* big-league careers.

Now, no one's out to argue that Ty Cobb was a power hitter as we'd define the term. But he did hit more home runs, and produce more runs, than people generally acknowledge.

Cobb led his league in runs batted in for four out of five years between 1907 and 1911. He also managed to hit twelve home runs twice during the course of his career. In no year did he *fail* to hit at least one home run, which is an achievement that eluded a great many of his contemporaries.

Despite Cobb's intimidating and highly competitive style of play, his extraordinary hitting ability, and his gargantuan ego, no team on which he played ever won a World Series. The Tigers teams on which he starred captured pennants in 1907, 1908, and 1909, but they did not emerge as World Champions. If, as Leo Durocher observed, nice guys do finish last, it's nevertheless comforting to note that talented, but psychopathic, misanthropes don't necessarily wind up on the top of the heap, either.

In summary: Even though nine round-trippers may not sound like a lot to us, leading the majors in home runs is leading the majors in home runs, and Cobb did it. (On the topic of the sometimes bewildering variations in the home-run totals of league leaders during the pre-Ruth period, see Myth 36.) He also hit more home runs over the course of his career than many people realize.

MYTH 19

Outfielder Paul Hines Pulled an Unassisted Triple Play

Three outs were recorded—that's hardly disputed—
But the facts of this gem are reconstituted.

An unassisted triple play—by an outfielder? How does this happen?

Well, Providence Grays left fielder Paul Hines supposedly knew all about it. He was the one who has been credited with turning this virtually unbelievable feat during a major-league game. If it were true, this play would be among the most remarkable defensive plays in major-league history, on a par with Cleveland infielder Bill Wambsgnass's unassisted triple play in the fifth game of the 1920 World Series against Brooklyn. But don't break out the champagne just yet.

A triple play *did* take place, but it's almost certain that Hines should be credited with two putouts, rather than three. Take a deep breath and pull out a pencil and paper. This gets a little involved.

What happened? Well, during an 1878 home game against Boston, Hines was playing left field; Boston's Jack Manning was on third and Ezra Sutton was on second. The batter, Jack Burdock, hit a ball to left field on which Hines made a superb play, snagging the ball from the tops of his shoes. One out.

Hines then scampered to third base—where runner Jack Manning wasn't—to make the second out.

This is where things get tricky. Those who argue that Hines secured all three putouts claim that, *before Hines made his catch*, Sutton, the man on second, had crossed third base—and by a fair length, because he failed to return to the bag in time. In support of this idea, people who want to credit Hines with all three putouts claim an ambiguous passage in the next day's paper about both runners "proceed(ing) to home plate," ignoring the obvious possibility that the writer was simply indicating the direction, and not the position, of the runners.

If Sutton did run from second to home before the catch, Hines would in fact have completed his unassisted triple play. But Hines's would not have been the most remarkable event of the day. Credit for that would have to go to Sutton for disproving many of our most cherished modern notions about the inability of any object to exceed the speed of light. The baserunner would have thus made impossible some of Albert Einstein's later conclusions on relativity, but that's a moot point. Suffice it to say that no completely human being could have covered the ground Sutton would have had to cover to make it well past third before Hines squeezed the ball, and that divine or interstellar intervention in the play seems unlikely.

Final key point: Everyone agrees that, after stepping on third base and retiring Manning, Hines threw to second. Why else would he have done that, if not to put out Sutton? For safety's sake, argue the proponents of the unassisted triple play.

Right.

It was a triple play—and it sounds like it was an exquisite one to watch—but it wasn't unassisted. Credit the final putout to Providence second baseman Charlie Sweasy.

In summary: Hines's heads-up play made the TP possible, but it didn't constitute a solo act. This one is a case of after-the-fact wishful thinking on the part of people who wanted to take one magical moment—a Hines-Sweasy triple play—and hammer it into an even *more* magical moment—a Hines triple play—that certainly would have been cool, if it could be argued into existence. But it can't. By the same token, the ball-and-strike counts in Yankee Don Larsen's 1956 perfect game against the Dodgers in the World Series can't be reassessed in such a way as to allow the Bronx Bombers' hurler to have struck out every batter he faced, even though that would have been really neat if it had actually taken place. Them's the breaks. Larsen did something amazing that requires no embellishment; so did Hines. Let's leave it at that. (For another account of an unusual defensive play that has oft been marred in the retelling, see Myth 43.)

MYTH 18

Babe Ruth Was a Draft Dodger

Was the Babe on the run 'cause the war made him nervous?
Did he pitch somewhere else to get out of the service?

In the fateful year of 1918, the Boston Red Sox beat the Chicago Cubs for the championship of the world. Among Boston's players that year was a man who would forever change the dimensions of the game: Babe Ruth.

Ruth served as both pitcher *and* position player that year (see Myth 12 for a discussion of his accomplishments during that remarkable "transition" season), and posted good numbers in both capacities. But the regular season was not without controversy for the promising youngster. During that year, a storm of press coverage settled on him—not for the last time—and Boston's versatile player came out looking less than patriotic. What happened? And why do some people still claim that the Babe was trying to pull a fast one with the draft board during this season?

The United States entered World War I in 1917; by 1918, there was talk of drafting major-league players who had not been called up under the "work-or-fight" order, which dictated that draftable young men who were engaged in "nonproductive" occupations were subject to the call even if they had been previously deferred. In July of 1918, Babe Ruth, a married man and a reservist who had been deferred, left the Red Sox and started talking to people at the Chester Shipyards about how much he might make by pitching for the shipyard ballclub. At the time, things were not going well between Ruth and his field commander—at Fenway Park.

It looked to many as though the Babe was trying to shield himself from the provisions of the "work-or-fight" decree by playing for a defense-related operation. But he *didn't* play. And if Ruth was so concerned about the decree, how are we to explain his return to the Boston club later in the same season, during a time when ballplayers were not subject to any special exemption from the draft? (A number were ordered into new jobs as a result of the work-or-fight edict.)

It appears that Ruth's brief departure from the Red Sox had more to do with his disputes with Boston manager Ed Barrow than it did with the war. Ruth never came to terms with the shipyard team; he did, however, come to terms with the Red Sox. Boston officials eventually got the Babe back and ignored a fine that Barrow had assessed against the lively young ballplayer.

Ruth's temporary absence from the Red Sox led to a lot of overblown newspaper stories, and the "draft-dodging" anecdote has come up from time to time over the years as a result. Was the Babe tough to manage? No one would dispute it. Did he play for a shipyard in order to keep from having to fight the good fight during World War I? Nope.

An interesting side note: The 1918 season came to an early conclusion as a result of wartime restrictions. That year's World Series, in which Boston triumphed for the last time (as of this writing), was more of a Late Summer Classic than a Fall Classic; play began on September 5, the earliest-ever starting date for a Series. As for Ruth, he won two games, posted a 1.06 earned-run average, and batted .200 as both a pitcher and an outfielder. He didn't hit a home run during the Series, but nobody else did, either.

In summary: The Bambino only *negotiated* with the Chester
Shipyards, and stories that he left the team in order to do so
because of the possibility of being drafted all tend to ignore
the "communication problems" (as we might put it euphe-
mistically today) between Ruth and his manager. In any
event, Ruth made it back to the team. He not only returned
to Boston and finished off a nice season as a pitcher,
outfielder, and first baseman, but he did so under the
distinct possibility that he might be drafted.

MYTH 17

The Boston Braves Were Named in Honor of the Disguised Raiders of the Boston Tea Party

These days, the Braves' name makes some people cringe,
But the moniker's not from the Tea Party binge.

What's in a name? Plenty, as it turns out.

Take the team name of the Atlanta Braves, for instance. The Braves logo, which of course appears on team uniforms, equipment, stationery, and promotional materials, has been met with a good deal of controversy in recent years, thanks to vocal protests from Native American groups. The contention that the team's name is racist picked up a good deal of media attention during the 1995 World Series, when the Braves met—and defeated—the Cleveland Indians, another team whose name has aroused protest from the same groups. Similar protests were heard during the Braves' earlier appearances in the Fall Classic.

The Braves' name, of course, dates back to its earlier incarnation as the Boston Braves. (Between its stays in Boston and Atlanta, the franchise spent over a decade in Milwaukee, and boasts the unusual distinction of having won world championships in three different cities.) However they feel about the charge of racism as it relates to the Braves' team name, most baseball fans have assumed that the name's origin derives from its Boston days, and that it was inspired, long after the fact, by that fair city's famed Tea Party of 1773.

The Tea Party, you may remember, was a colonial act of defiance against English taxation policies. Three tea ships arrived in Boston, and the British governor refused to let the ships leave harbor before they coughed up the required cash. On the night of December 16, 1773, a band of furious colonists—among them Samuel Adams and Paul Revere—dressed up as Indians, boarded the ships, and tossed the tea overboard. The incident was one of the most famous precursors to the American Revolution, and its retelling for generations in the nation's elementary-school history classes insured that the city of Boston would forever be associated with the image of (ersatz) Indians.

All that would *seem* to lead to the conclusion that the National League team took on the name "Boston Braves" in 1912 in memory of that hallowed night of rabble-rousing. But in fact the team's name was chosen because its owner, Jim Gaffney, was a high official in the Tammany Hall political machine, which patterned its organization and titles after supposed Native American rituals. The Tammany Society, which was founded in the 1780s and came to dominate New York City politics utterly in the latter part of the nineteenth century, divided itself into thirteen "tribes." Gaffney was a chieftain.

Before they were known as the Braves, Boston's National League franchise was known as the Red Stockings, the Beaneaters, and the Doves. The name instituted under Gaffney, however, stuck—even when the team underwent a disastrous 38–115 finish in 1935 and tried, for a few years, to change its name to the Bees. The idea didn't make much of a buzz, and the team eventually reverted to the familiar Braves name.

For the record, the Cleveland Indians' team nickname was adopted as an homage to one of the most beloved players in the team's history, not as a jab at Native Americans. The team was known as the Spiders when Louis Sockalexis, a Penobscot Indian, joined them in 1897. Manager John McGraw considered Sockalexis the greatest natural talent yet seen on the diamond. Sockalexis was a great crowd favorite, and he played well for Cleveland, compiling a .313 average over three seasons. But he was a heavy drinker, and that problem led to the end of his major-league career. Two years after Sockalexis's early death in 1913, the fans of Cleveland paid him tribute by renaming the franchise the Indians in a vote sponsored by a local newspaper. (In earlier days, the team had been known as the Naps, a nod to player-manager Napoleon Lajoie.)

The origins of both the Atlanta and the Cleveland team names are not well known, despite the ongoing controversy about their current use. Some would argue that the beginnings don't really matter, and that it is only the *effect* of the names on those who hear them that matters. As of this writing, however, neither franchise appears eager to institute a name change, and the entire topic seems likely to be filed under "something to talk about" for the forseeable future.

In summary: The Braves' name is the result of its owner's prominence in the Tammany Hall machine, not the famed Boston guerrilla assault on ships bearing tea.

MYTH 16

Female Baseball Players Have Never Competed Against Men on the Professional Level

Two women made breakthroughs not often recorded,
And their efforts deserve to be duly reported.

We're not talking about exhibition games here (Babe Didrikson pitched against big-leaguers during an unofficial contest). The question is whether a female player ever took her place among men in organized, professional, regular-season games, in male-dominated leagues. And the answer, despite what you may hear from time to time via the sports news media, is yes. At least two female players did have modest professional debuts on male teams.

Two may not *sound* like a lot—and the sight of women players on a big-league ballfield may be a good many years off—but these two players certainly give the lie to the notion that female ballplayers are unheard of in the professional game. Perhaps their example will help a qualified woman player to gain a toehold in today's game. And by the way, does anyone recall the bitter protests of the 1970s against allowing female players to take part in Little League games? Remember the predictions that the republic would collapse, and that the experience would leave all involved—and, indeed, the Game Itself—scarred for life? Did any of that hold water?

Whether or not the presence of girls in present-day Little League games is a harbinger of things to come in professional baseball, the fact remains that there were two women who got paid to compete against men during the regular season. They didn't stick around for long, but they did take their place in the field.

Both of the events took place in the minors. A woman who went by the name of Lizzie Arlington (she was born Lizzie Stroud) pitched for the Reading team of the Atlantic League in 1898. Arlington was a member of the Bloomer Girls, a traveling all-female team that promoted her heavily, traveled in its "own special palace car" and, around the turn of the century, advertised an impressive 731–646 record over the past nine years. ("Truthfully advertised and honestly conducted," the team's handbill boasted. "Plenty of good seats and shade. A highclass organization suitable for the most fastidious. Come and bring the ladies. Patronized by every one.")

Arlington appears to have pitched in only one game in organized male ball, although there are unverified claims that she was a considerable gate attraction throughout that season. What is certain is that she came in and pitched part of an inning on July 5, 1898, and that no one scored a run against her.

The second woman known to have made the minors was one Frances Dunlap, who played right field for a full game in the Class-D Arkansas-Missouri League in 1936. She went 0-for-3 as a member of the Fayetteville Bears, and then seems to have dropped out of organized ball.

Will future women have the chance to make more of a splash in the minors—or perhaps even the big leagues? Only time will tell.

In summary: Lizzie Arlington and Frances Dunlap deserve to be recognized as women who made incursions—briefly—into a "man's game." It's worth noting that both of these events took place before the founding of the now-famous All-American Girls Professional Baseball League in the 1940s, whose exploits formed the basis of the movie *A League of Their Own.* Note: Although the much-ballyhooed all-female team the Silver Bullets has played against male teams in recent times, they have not done so as part of an organized professional league.

MYTH 15

Joe Nuxhall Was the Youngest Player Ever to Compete in the Big Leagues

Nuxhall made headlines, of that there's no doubt,
But Chapman still ranks as the youngest man out.

How many millions of kids in sandlot and Little League games have fantasized over the years about making it to the major leagues—dreamed of snatching the brass ring by means of perseverance, dedication, hard work, and, of course, a healthy dose of God-given natural talent? The actual number will never be known, but it's fair to say that it's huge, and that this youthful dream is among the most popular and enduring in the American psyche. Most, of course, don't make it, but then again, most kids who dream about becoming firefighters and construction workers find something else to do with their lives, too.

Now then—how many kids dream about making it to the big leagues, and then do, *while still children?*

Not too many. But their stories are fascinating.

There could have been any number of reasons the Cincinnati Reds decided to elevate pitcher Joe Nuxhall to the big leagues in 1944. Perhaps they liked his style. Perhaps they'd heard good things about his attitude on the mound. Then again, perhaps they were facing a wartime pitching shortage that left them short of warm bodies in the bullpen, and perhaps they were willing, on June 10 of that year, to see what would happen when they brought in a reliever who was a month and a half shy of his sixteenth birthday.

Nuxhall pitched two-thirds of an inning against the Cardinals and got bombed. He gave up five runs in his only appearance of the year, and posted a surrealistic earned-run average of 67.50 for the year.

It was your basic tough gig. Nuxhall received a good deal of press attention for his debut, and, although his traumatizing debut at the major-league level was discussed for years to come, he was *not* the youngest person ever to play in the big leagues. That honor goes to a fourteen-year-old by the name of Fred Chapman, who pitched five innings for Philadelphia's American Association team in 1887, his only outing of the season. Chapman closed out the year—and his career—with a 7.20 earned-run average.

Although Chapman never pitched again on the major-league level, Nuxhall returned (after an eight-year absence) to the Reds and followed through with a solid, sixteen-season record of big-league performance. He finished up with a lifetime winning record of 135–117; his best year was 1963, when he went 15–8 and posted a 2.61 earned-run average.

For both pitchers, the first season was difficult, to say the least...if, that is, you can call Nuxhall's brief 1944 appearance, and Chapman's slightly longer 1887 one "seasons." Yet unlike the younger Chapman, Nuxhall came back and built himself a career in baseball, for which he deserves a great deal of credit. Comparatively young "phee-noms" who are brought to the majors too early in their careers (like Texas's eighteen-year-old David Clyde, who tried and failed to craft a successful major-league career in the 1970s) usually find adult success in the big leagues to be an elusive goal indeed.

In summary: Not many teenagers make it to the big leagues, and fewer still thrive there. Fred Chapman was one of the players who didn't stick around. Although his big-league career was a brief one, and not in any way glorious, it deserves to be noted. He appears to be the youngest *professional* baseball player of all time—in other words, the youngest person ever to take the field for pay in the major or minor leagues.

MYTH 14

Pitcher Rube Waddell Dismissed His Outfielders During an Official Major-League Game and Went on to Retire the Side

The trick would have been grand...
And gotten him canned.

Outfielders? Who needs them?

Philadelphia Pitcher Rube Waddell, one of the most eccentric major-league players of all time, has frequently been credited with an extraordinary feat of pitching machismo (or foolishness); that of sending his outfielders to the bench during a regular-season game and retiring the side.

Waddell, whom Connie Mack considered "one of the best left-handers I ever saw," was certainly wacky. He wrestled alligators, spent money like it was water (an unfortunate habit for a professional ballplayer of his era), and reportedly delayed the starts of games in which he was supposed to pitch because he was busy playing with children outside the stadium. More than one of his teammates suspected that he was mentally unbalanced. Whether or not Waddell was certifiable, he was a powerhouse drinker of spiritous beverages whose alcohol-fueled on-field and off-field exploits were more than a little bizarre. Still, it's impossible to believe he could have gotten away with the stunt that has so often been attributed to him in any big-league game that could have affected the outcome of his team's standings. No reliable firsthand account of such an incident has surfaced.

The story seems to have been yet another case of a baseball legend feeding on itself. One of Waddell's teammates claimed that the Rube once managed to pull the "who-needs-the-outfielders" trick during an (unidentified) spring training game while he was pitching for the Pittsburgh Pirates. He also appears to have narrowly escaped disaster when he waved fielders to the dugout during an exhibition game in Memphis; after striking out two men, we are told, Waddell watched as his catcher, the only other defensive player on the field, dropped a third strike with two out, leading to two unfieldable fly balls from the next two batters. (Waddell supposedly struck out the final batter of the inning.) Then there's the story that tells how he once repositioned his fielders during a league game against Detroit, leaving the outfielders sitting on the grass near the infield, and then calmly proceeded to strike out the side.

Whether these events actually took place, and it's entirely possible that they did, they're each a far cry from the popular story that a big-league team—and that means the manager and at least three professional players—would have acquiesced to the idea of outfielders abandoning the field during a league game. Anyway, doing so is against the rules in official games: there must be nine men, somewhere, on the field. Umpires would only have allowed Waddell to get away with the dismissing-the-fielders stunt during exhibition contests.

A variation on the "sending-the-fielders-off-the-field" tale is also told about the legendary Negro League pitcher Satchel Paige, the flamboyant showmanship of whose league and era may well have been more conducive to such a display of pitching ability during league contests. Some versions of the Paige story swapped over barstools feature a confident Satch who, like Waddell in the story of the Memphis game, orders not only the outfielders, but also the *infielders* off the field, and then proceeds to strike out three straight batters.

It's certainly within the realm of possibility that *some* crowd-pleasing maneuver of Paige's lies beneath this version of the story, but the details are sketchy. Then again, lots of events that took place in the Negro Leagues remain sketchy. What's certain is that Paige was regarded by the top players of his time, both black and white, as one of the greatest pitchers who ever lived. (Joe DiMaggio called Paige "the best I've ever faced, and the fastest.")

As for Rube, he *was* overpowering on the mound: He posted a lifetime earned-run average of 2.16 (better than, for instance, that of Sandy Koufax), and struck out 349 batters in 1904, a record that stood until Nolan Ryan's day. (Note: Waddell's 1904 strikeout total was initially miscalculated at 343, an error that went uncorrected for decades.) He was also loopy, and he may well have been odd enough to *suggest* trying his no-outfielders routine during an official game. Until some documented regular-season reference to the extraordinary feat attributed to him shows up, however, this one's best filed under "pass the salt shaker."

In summary: Plenty of stories have been told about Rube Waddell, and most of them accent both his confidence and his eccentricity. Although these qualities were undeniably in evidence during his strange and storied major-league career, the no-outfielders trick *couldn't* have happened under major-league rules during a regular league game. Waddell's general strangeness—which was considerable—probably led to a significant exaggeration of a story that may be based on something he did during an exhibition contest.

MYTH 13

The World Champion 1991 Minnesota Twins Posted the Greatest Worst-to-First Record of All Time

Last place to first—an incredible feat.
But the Twins, in this case, aren't the outfit to beat.

Far be it from me to detract from the achievements of the '91 Twins. They were an extraordinary team.

Having concluded the 1990 season with a 74–88 record that left them 29 games back of the front-running A's and in sole possession of the American League West cellar, the Twins managed a remarkable comeback in 1991. They won 95, outdistanced the second-place Chicago White Sox by 8 full games, beat the Toronto Blue Jays for the pennant in 5, and then embarked on a scintillating 7-game World Series against the Atlanta Braves—who had also wound up 1990 in last place. The series ended in victory for Minnesota, with Dan Gladden scoring in the bottom of the tenth of a scoreless Game Seven. In one year, the Twins had gone from being a doormat to being the world champions, and (based on their play in the Series) probably the most exciting team in the game.

The former cellar-dwellars from Minnesota made baseball amazing again in 1991. But theirs was not, as many

people have come to believe, the most remarkable turn-
around in the game's history.

Not even a World Series occupied by *two* last-place
finishers from the previous year can eclipse the accomplishment of the 1914 Boston Braves. The year before, they had
posted an abysmal 69–82 record, and not long after the 1914
season began they found themselves in last place, a position
they began to settle into with disconcerting ease. They
stayed in the cellar for three straight months.

The Braves' 1914 season seemed to be going nowhere but
down. Manager George Stallings described his team as
"...one .300 hitter, the worst outfield that ever flirted with
sudden death, three pitchers, and a good working combination around second base." Stallings set his sights on a fifth-
place finish and hoped he wouldn't get fired at the end of the
year.

Then, in mid-July, an odd thing happened. The Boston
Braves began winning baseball games.

The lineup—sparked by outfielder Joe Connolly, shortstop Rabbit Maranville, and first baseman Butch Schmidt—
finally started producing enough runs to support the starting pitching rotation. And the pitchers responded. A
twenty-two-year-old righty by the name of Bill James, 8–6 in
the middle of July, caught fire in the second half, posting a
nearly unbelievable 18–1 record the rest of the way. His ERA
at year's end was a microscopic 1.90. Midway through the
year, right-hander Dick Rudolph was the owner of a 10–9
record. He ended the season with 27 victories—tops in the
National League—and only 10 losses. His end-of-season
ERA: 2.35.

Midway through the 1914 season the Boston Braves were
a self-destructing last-place team with little hope of finishing anywhere outside of the second division. They went on
to post what must be the most spectacular second half in
baseball history, winning 61 of their final 77 contests, and

briskly eliminating the flabbergasted New York Giants—the reigning National League champions—from the pennant race.

The Braves won the pennant by *ten and a half games*. They went on to sweep the previous year's world champions, the Philadelphia Athletics, in the World Series.

The worst team in the league had emerged as the best in all of baseball, and it had done so, not as the result of off-season regrouping, but *between the months of July and October*, with the whole sporting world watching gapemouthed.

What the Braves did in 1914 was—and is likely to remain—unparalleled. They reinvented themselves on the spot. They turned the expectations of the baseball world upside down in the process by systematically dismantling the two powerhouses of the day: the New York Giants and the Philadelphia Athletics. Until another team rises from the bottom of the heap to claim not just a World Series victory, but a *decisive* World Series victory, within a span of less than four months, the '14 Braves must be recognized as baseball's ultimate worst-to-first story.

In summary: The '91 Twins may have earned glory for their memorable victory in the World Series of that year—and perhaps even proved that their victory in the '87 Fall Classic was no fluke, despite that squad's mediocre 85–77 regular season record—but Minnesota didn't hit the high mark on the all-time jaw-dropping meter for big-league baseball. (Nor, for that matter, did the '93 Phillies, who managed to win the National League pennant after finishing last in 1992, only to drop the Series to the Toronto Blue Jays.) The ultimate worst-to-first team was the gloriously improbable 1914 Boston Braves.

MYTH 12

Boston Manager Ed Barrow's Decision to Move Babe Ruth Into the Outfield Was a Stroke of Genius

Was Barrow the mastermind? That's the contention.
But necessity—and Hooper—set up his invention.

Babe Ruth's transition from (superb) pitcher to (revolutionary) everyday player is probably one of the most important single events in the history of big-league baseball. By 1919, the transition was complete, and Ruth hit 29 home runs as a regular. The seeds for that pivotal season had been planted the year before.

Boston manager Ed Barrow, who made the call in that paid off big in 1918, is often credited with one of the shrewdest managerial moves in the game's history: taking that hard-swinging Ruth fellow off the mound and getting his bat into the lineup more often than once or twice a week.

Fateful, maybe. Shrewd, no.

Barrow apparently wasn't crazy about changing Ruth's position. This is understandable; the Babe had led the Sox in victories and had posted an ERA of 2.01 in the previous year. In other words, he was the ace of the staff. Why mess around with a good thing?

The reason Ruth saw duty as an outfielder and first

baseman in 1918 was simple: Boston didn't have enough quality outfielders, thanks to the departure of a good many ballplayers into the service after the outbreak of World War I. Evidently it was Boston outfielder Harry Hooper who prevailed on Barrow to turn the Babe into an everyday player. Hooper, who was elected to the Hall of Fame in 1971, had been part of Boston's famous (and, given the salaries of the day, fancifully named) "Million Dollar Outfield"; the other stars were Tris Speaker and Duffy Lewis. Hooper was the Red Sox' leadoff hitter during their glory years in the 'teens. In the 1915 World Series, Harry Hooper became the first man to hit two home runs in a single World Series game. (Ruth would manage the trick in 1923, and then hit *three* in a single Series game in 1926.)

From the record as it now stands, it seems likely that the Babe would never have put in the time at first base and in the outfield that he did in 1918 if the Red Sox' roster hadn't been depleted as a result of the war, and if Harry Hooper hadn't had the presence of mind to mention the idea to Ed Barrow. One thing's for certain; the decision to get more out of Ruth's bat led to a lot of noise around Fenway. And he *did* still pitch in twenty games.

Ruth's statistics for the Red Sox' championship year are a great deal of fun to look at.

As a batter: Ruth came to the plate 317 times, hit an even .300, and led the league in home runs and slugging percentage.

As a pitcher: Ruth went 13–7, posted a 2.22 earned-run average, and completed eighteen of his twenty starts. All this in a year in which he went AWOL for a part of the season! (See Myth 18.)

Like many another more or less desperate improvisation that looked pretty darn good after the dust settled, Barrow's move has been hailed as inspired. It was nothing of the sort. If anyone deserves the credit for transforming the twenty-three-year-old Ruth into an everyday player, it's Harry Hooper.

In summary: Ruth's transition had more to do with Harry Hooper and the Great War than any great brainstorm on Ed Barrow's part. If Barrow's work during the 1918 season is to be remembered, it should be because he piloted the Boston Red Sox to victory in the World Series. He was, as this is being written, the last man to do that. Boston's championship drought has extended over the past seventy-eight years as this book goes to press.

MYTH 11

Philadelphia First Baseman
Al Reach Was the First Professional
Baseball Player

Getting cash to play ball? What an etiquette breach!
The first to get paid sure wasn't Al Reach.

It hardly seems possible now to imagine a time when the most talented players accepted no cash for playing the game, but such were the beginnings of baseball.

The amateur status of the ballclubs of the 1860s was a matter of pride—and controversy. When teams used cold, hard cash to lure a player away from another outfit, purists saw red. As a result, actually *paying* ballplayers to do their thing on the diamond was something teams did on the sly. (Today's astronomical salaries, even adjusted for a century-plus of inflation, would probably have convinced baseball fans of the Civil War era that the nation had gone certifiably insane.)

Because of the emphasis on amateurism during this period, and the attendant secrecy accompanying pay arrangements for the ballplayers of the day, there's been some confusion about the identity of the very first professional ballplayer. For a good many years, the player was thought to be left-handed outfielder/second-baseman Al Reach, who got twenty-five dollars per week to play for the Philadelphia Athletics in 1865. (The cash was supposedly meant to defray "expenses.") From time to time, you still hear his name in this context. Reach, who was born in England and made his name as a ballplayer in Brooklyn, New York, seems to have been one of a number of players Philadelphia paid "under the table" during this period.

Fortunately for the American sporting world's sense of national pride, American-born Jim Creighton must, in the absence of new evidence, be regarded as the first professional baseball player. He should probably be regarded as the game's first real superstar, as well.

We know that the Brooklyn Excelsiors paid Creighton— quietly—to pitch for them as early as 1860. His speedy delivery and subtle wrist twist made him one of the most formidable hurlers of the day. Creighton was a very popular player, and his death, which came about as the result of a mysterious "internal injury" incurred while swinging at a pitch during a game, was mourned by the game's growing legions of fans. The large granite monument above Creighton's grave in Brooklyn's Greenwood Cemetery incorporates a ball, a baseball cap, a pair of crossed bats, and a scorebook.

The Excelsiors may well have paid other "amateurs" on their roster for playing the game. What is certain is that they paid Creighton, and thus it is Creighton, not Reach, who deserves to be acknowledged as the first confirmed professional ballplayer.

Reach went on to start a sporting goods outfit that made him a very rich man; he sold the business to A. G. Spalding in 1889, but stayed on as an executive. He also founded an annual baseball publication that helped to increase fan interest in the statistical side of the game.

Creighton, in death, took his place as the first of a long line of star-crossed Brooklyn heroes.

In summary: Big Jim Creighton, not Al Reach, should be regarded as the first professional baseball player.

MYTH 10

In 1947, the St. Louis Cardinals Seriously Considered Going on Strike Rather Than Face Brooklyn's Jackie Robinson on the Playing Field

The Cardinals made ominous headlines, we know,
But they didn't conspire to shut down the show.

The New York *Herald-Tribune* "broke" the story that led the world to believe that the St. Louis Cardinals had been on the verge of refusing to take the field against the Brooklyn Dodgers—and black player Jackie Robinson—during the early part of the 1947 season. The whole brouhaha appears to have been an inspired rumor-enhancement operation conducted by a newspaper in pursuit of a hot story.

In other words, there may well have been some loose talk in the Cardinal clubhouse about sitting out games against Brooklyn, but there is slim proof indeed that it ever took the form of an organized effort to keep the team from competing when Robinson took the field. The *Herald-Tribune* seems to have taken the St. Louis owner's understandable concern about occasional mutterings about playing on the same field with Robinson—mutterings that were by no means unique to the Cardinal locker room—as inspiration for a power-

....

house story, and then used exaggerated reports of a Cardinal uprising to encourage National League president Ford Frick to issue a statement on the matter.

Before the story broke, Cardinal owner Sam Breadon had been assured by player representatives Marty Marion and Terry Moore that no strike was in the offing. Once the *Herald-Tribune* weighed in with its version of events, the two teams had already completed a 3-game series that went off without a trace of the nonexistent St. Louis walkout. The strike story nevertheless managed to win headlines in the following days.

The exaggerations around the supposed strike in St. Louis don't stop there. It has often been claimed that Cardinal star Stan Musial got into a fistfight with Enos Slaughter over Robinson and the Dodgers. There's only one problem with this story: at the time the event is supposed to have occurred, Musial was either under hospital care for, or recuperating from, an attack of appendicitis.

Lots of National League players (and managers) had misgivings about playing against Robinson. They generally took out these sentiments by the more direct method of attempting to injure him on the field of play. The supposed uprising by St. Louis players bears all the hallmarks of a made-to-order story designed to capitalize on the Robinson phenomenon. It worked.

In summary: A few Cardinals may have been flapping their jaws about playing against Robinson, but the team appears *not* to have been ready to take on the major-league establishment en masse.

MYTH 9

The First Big-League Designated Hitter in a Regular Season Game Came to Bat in 1973

Cutting some corners? Perhaps. All the same,
The White Sox were decades ahead of the game.

Although the ideas for a designated-hitter rule had been kicking around for decades (see Myth 47), baseball didn't get around to formalizing the notion of a permanent hitter to stand in for the pitcher until 1973, when the American League started playing under the system. That's not to say, however, that there *were* no designated hitters in big-league ball before that date. There's at least one instance on record of a game that was played using a DH—illegally, but with big-league baseball nevertheless accepting the resulting statistics—in 1939.

The contest took place in Chicago, where the White Sox were playing the Cleveland Indians. During the game, White Sox manager Jimmy Dykes approached Cleveland skipper Oskar Vitt and asked him whether the Chicago pitcher, Bill Dietrich, could be allowed to remain in the contest *after* Dykes sent up a pinch hitter for him. The open-minded Cleveland manager replied that *he* had no problem with the arrangement as long as the *umpires* had no problem with it.

....

The necessary discussions were concluded, a pinch-hitter batted for Dietrich, and Dykes continued to pitch!

There appear to have been a number of "informal" designated-hitter arrangements along these lines in the years before the American League settled on the rule for good in 1973. Whether formal acceptance of the DH rule represented a natural and healthy accommodation to fans who enjoy high-scoring games, or an unwarranted assault on the game's fundamental structure, remains a matter of debate.

The Dietrich story is recounted in Robert Obojski's fine book *Baseball's Strangest Moments*.

In summary: The designated-hitter rule has at least one (informal) precedent before its 1973 debut in the American League.

MYTH 8

Ray Chapman's Death Led to the Abolition of the Spitball

Did the Chapman case lead to a ban on spitters?
Nope. The dates don't match up. Credit the hitters.

Robert Coover's fine book *The Universal Baseball Association, J. Henry Waugh, Prop.*, features an imaginary table-game league, run by a baseball-mad accountant. Among the early plot twists: the loss of a promising young pitcher named Damon Rutherford at the plate when a toss of the dice leads to a beanball pitch that fatally strikes the budding—and imaginary—star. The accountant starts to come unglued.

Coover's extraordinary fictional account of a death at the plate (or is that on the chart?) may well have been inspired by an all-too-real incident from a pivotal year in big-league baseball.

One of the greatest tragedies in the history of the major leagues was the death of Cleveland shortstop Ray Chapman, who in later years was hailed as the type of ballplayer who might very well have made the Hall of Fame had he not been cut down by a pitch from Yankee hurler Carl Mays. Chapman hit .312 in his rookie year of 1912, led the American League in runs scored in 1918, and led his own team in stolen bases four times. His mark of 52 swipes in 1917 stood as a team record until 1980.

....

Chapman, who was batting .303 at the time of his death, was struck in the head by a delivery from Mays on August 16, 1920, in New York. He had been crowding the plate, and by all accounts did not make an attempt to move out of the path of Mays's pitch, which was near the strike zone. The impact of the blow was so loud that the ball was fielded and thrown to first. The defensive players believed that the ball had been struck by Chapman's bat.

To date, Chapman is the only major-league player to die as the direct and immediate result of an injury during the course of a game.

Because the fatal beaning came about in the fateful year of 1920—the same year that big-league baseball outlawed trick pitches such as the spitball—many have held that the Cleveland shortstop's death *brought about* the ban on the sneaky pitches.

It's easy to see how someone might come to that conclusion: Chapman died as the result of a pitch to the head. Some of the pitches that end up hitting people in the head are pitches that are unpredictable or out of control. Spitballs, scuffballs, emery balls, and the rest all have a tendency to dance around uncontrollably. Thus, Chapman's death probably had something to do with the ban on the trick pitches.

It all seems sensible enough, but the truth is that the doctored balls were outlawed—for all but a few hurlers whose careers depended on them—at the *beginning* of the 1920 season, not after Chapman's death. The last legal spitball was thrown in 1934 by Burleigh Grimes, one of the chosen few permitted to retain his bread-and-butter pitch in his repertoire.

The real reason the trick pitches were banned was simple: Baseball executives wanted to change the way baseball was played. They wanted to see more runs on the board, and spitballs were too hard to hit. The baseball authorities also instituted a new, livelier ball. Batting averages and home-run totals soared.

The Chapman tragedy *did* help to bring about a new practice in baseball, that of quickly removing marked or scuffed balls from the game and replacing them with clean, new white ones that are easier to spot.

The Cleveland team, which wore black armbands in Chapman's honor, went on to win both the American League pennant and the first World Series title in the club's history. Chapman's replacement, Joe Sewell, played 22 games at shortstop that year, and eventually emerged as a major star in his own right, compiling a .312 lifetime batting average and winning a spot in the Hall of Fame in 1971.

Carl Mays, who won 21 games for the world champion 1918 Red Sox, was one of the great Boston players who migrated to the Yankees during the late teens. He was nicknamed "Sub" for his submarine-style pitching technique. Mays, an unflappable sort, was never prosecuted for his role in the Chapman beaning, although he was taunted mercilessly about the incident by the ever-sensitive Ty Cobb. Chapman played nine more years in the majors. Proof that he did not let the incident interfere unduly with his approach to the game can be found in the 1921 season that followed the beaning, which was the best of Chapman's career. He led the American league in victories in 1921 with 26, and threw in seven saves and a 3.05 earned-run average for good measure. Over the course of his fifteen-year career, Mays won 20 or more games in five seasons, and boasted a career mark of 208 victories against only 126 defeats.

There have been other unfortunate beanings in the major leagues since Chapman, but no fatalities arising from a batter being hit by a pitch. Mickey Cochrane, one of the all-time great receivers, was struck by a pitched ball in 1937 and very nearly died; he survived, however, and, although his career as a player was through, he did return to the game as a successful manager. Joe Medwick was beaned in 1940 in his first at-bat for the Brooklyn Dodgers, to whom he had recently been traded. Red Sox slugger Tony Conigliaro was never the same after being struck by a pitch in 1967; nor was Houston shortstop Dickie Thon, whose vision was damaged when he was beaned in 1984.

In summary: The ban on trick pitches did not come about as the result of big-league baseball management's care and compassion for the game's players, but for a less inspiring reason: The owners wanted to make more money, and they thought that higher-scoring games would pack people into the stands in greater numbers. They were right. The banning of the spitball and its legion of companion "doctored" pitches was just part of the movement to tilt the game in the direction of the batter rather than the pitcher.

MYTH 7

The Cincinnati Red Stockings Were the First Professional Baseball Team

The Cincinnati team had plenty of dash,
But it wasn't the first to play for hard cash.

Let's be clear on one thing: the landmark 1869 Cincinnati Red Stockings, composed of twelve ballplayers assembled by Harry Wright, appear to have been the first *openly* professional team. But pressures to excel at the increasingly popular game had led more than one team to pay its players under the table long before 1869. (See Myth 11.)

In his book *Baseball Between the Lies*, author Bob Carroll makes an intriguing reference to a contemporary report of an 1864 game between New York and Brooklyn in which spectators were charged an admission fee of ten cents—the proceeds being divided equally among the players. Carroll points out that, if the incident did in fact take place, and if all members of both teams received shares, then it's hard to see why the New York Mutuals and Brooklyn Atlantics shouldn't be considered to have been playing professionally at the time.

Even if the 1864 game is set aside from the argument for some reason, the fact remains that a good many teams were paying players to take the field before 1869 in the hopes of putting together the best possible squad. Exactly how many players were being paid, how much they received, and what kind of disparities existed between "true" amateur outfits and "false" ones are all very murky questions indeed. (When people break the rules, they generally don't make a habit of boasting about it.) But most historians agree that pay-for-play arrangements were an open secret by the late 1860s, and the excuses some teams made to justify their amateur status were often very thin ones indeed.

The Red Stockings deserve their place in baseball history not because no one had ever been paid to play baseball before—lots of people had—but because the team's forthright approach to the issue of professionalism led to new, if not always unanimous, respect and interest from the fans. People knew they were coming to see the best ballclub Harry Wright could pay to put together, and the unconvincing charade that top teams were composed of players who were only "gentlemen athletes" could finally stop.

The Cincinnati team also deserves its place in baseball history because it was very, very good. Wright's open embrace of professionalism, even though it was decried by purists, paid off in spades. Cincinnati played all opponents and won its first 60 games of the season. It spun off 30 straight victories the next year.

And if you've ever referred to a team's top pitcher as its "ace," you're paying a compliment to an original member of the Red Stockings' lineup. The word springs from the nickname that Cincinnati pitcher Asa Brainard first made popular in baseball circles. Brainard, also known as "Count," went on to pitch for the Washington Olympians and for other teams in the National Association, but his lifetime record in this early league was an uninspiring 24 victories and 56 losses. His glory days had been with the Red Stockings.

Brainard's old team was a breakthrough outfit, and an exciting, virtually unbeatable squad in 1869 and 1870, but it wasn't the first to feature paid ballplayers.

In summary: If you have to have a team (or two) to point to when it comes to identifying the first assembly of professional ballplayers, the reported 1864 game between Brooklyn and New York may be just what you're looking for. As far as the Red Stockings go, there's a distinction to be made between the first *openly* pro team (which it was), and the first team to pay money to its players (which it wasn't).

MYTH 6

Abner Doubleday Invented the Game of Baseball in the Summer of 1839

Cooperstown may boast of the Hall of Fame,
But it isn't the burg that gave birth to the game.

Question before the house: What was the name of the man who "invented" baseball?

Perhaps the best way to respond is to answer the question by posing another: Who "invented" chess? Or the Bible? Or the I Ching? Or rock-and-roll?

The origins of all of these things were gradual affairs, and all can be said to possess certain rhythms, complexities, and idiosyncracies that are the result of many guiding hands, and constant experimentation and elaboration over time.

Something recognizably similar to the game we know and love today had emerged by the middle of the nineteenth century; we may choose to call that something "baseball," but it was not the result of a flash of inspiration on the part of one person.

Certain elements of the American baseball establishment didn't want to hear that back in the 1900s, however.

There is a natural human tendency to want to be able to say, "Baseball started right here, and at this particular time." And there's a decided *American* tendency to want to be able to say, "Baseball was something that was invented in this country, by an American." But the truth is a little more complex.

Baseball's Hall of Fame is, as good baseball fans know, situated in the quaint village of Cooperstown, New York. This municipality is (or so the story went) the town where Abner Doubleday established the major principles of the game in 1839. The origin of this information? A commission was formed with the stated purpose of determining the true beginnings of the game of baseball. A. G. Mills, former president of the National League, led the group. He submitted his final report in December of 1907.

The report was supposed to clear up all those pesky lingering questions. Mills was the first to attribute the origin of the game of baseball to Doubleday, an American who had fought at the Battle of Gettysburg and who happened to be conveniently dead.

Hmm...

For support, Mills called on the account of a man named Abner Graves, who claimed to have been present at the fateful 1839 game—as a child of five years of age with, presumably, an excellent memory. Mr. Graves turned out to be the only person who ever spoke of actually witnessing Doubleday on a baseball field. What's more, the witness's credibility may be worth considering closely, given his life's general instability. Graves shot his wife—she died as a result—and he was, by the end of his life, a resident of an institution for the criminally insane. An old baseball found in Graves's things was hailed as the Sacred Doubleday Ball, but no reliable documentation connecting it to Doubleday or the year 1839 has ever surfaced.

Hmm...

Later research has shown that Doubleday was at West Point during the time he was supposed to have been at Cooperstown devising the National Pastime. He made no claim of having invented the game of baseball. He also kept dozens of diaries, not a one of which mentions the game.

Hmm...

Doubleday's connection with the game was a hoax perpetrated by patriotic American bigwigs who couldn't abide the idea that the game of baseball derived from the British games of cricket and rounders. But it did, and it did so gradually, over a period of years, not all at once on a single glorious day. All the same, a good many baseball fans are still under the misimpression that Doubleday invented the game.

In summary: Visit Cooperstown because it's a pleasant town that happens to have become the repository for the collection of baseball's most important memorabilia, because it boasts plaques that honor the greatest players in the game's history, and because it is the site of the annual Hall of Fame game played every summer at quaint Doubleday Field. If any of the locals try to tell you that the town is the birthplace of the game of baseball, smile pleasantly and change the subject.

MYTH 5

Dizzy Dean Won 30 Games in 1934

The Diz was a trickster, no doubt about that:
One '34 win came straight out of his hat.

Look under *colorful* in the Great Baseball Dictionary, and you're likely to see a photograph of the Detroit ace of the 1930s.

Jay Hanna "Dizzy" Dean was a brash, overbearing, utterly unforgettable pitcher who came from a small town in Arkansas. He was a traveling cotton-picker when he was discovered by the Cardinal farm system at a tryout. When he won a spot as a player in organized baseball, he had not finished any form of school past the second grade.

Dean made the big-league team after he claimed to Cardinal boss Branch Rickey that he could fill more seats than Babe Ruth. Such self-confidence was the Arkansan's hallmark, and he put it to good use, assembling five sterling seasons with the Cardinals, including the dream year of 1934. In that memorable season, as all the authorities inform us, Dean hammered through for 30 wins, the last major leaguer to hit that pinnacle until Denny McLain's 1968 season with the Tigers.

All the authorities are wrong. Confidence or no confidence, Dean won only 29 games in 1934.

On June 27, he was credited with a victory that should

have gone to somebody else. Dean, who had been pitching as a reliever, was awarded the win despite the fact that the guiding scoring rules of the day should have granted the victory to Cardinal pitcher Jim Mooney. The scoring mistake is noted in David Nemec's book *Great Baseball Feats, Facts, and Firsts*.

To be sure, Dean did some amazing things during the 1934 season, not the least of which was his follow-through on his brash prediction that he and his brother Paul would combine for at least 45 wins that year. The promise seemed absurd, as Paul had yet to pitch in the big leagues, but the two made good on Diz's word—even removing the controversial June 27 decision, the pair was good for 48 victories—and then set the baseball world on its ear during the World Series against the Tigers. Each sibling won 2 games during that Fall Classic.

But as great as he was during the memorable 1934 season, the 30-win plateau actually eluded Dean, as it has many a gifted pitcher before and since. McLain, as of this writing, is the only big-leaguer to break through the barrier since Dean's day.

How big a deal is that? Well, it doesn't change the fact that Dean was the pitcher teams hated to hit against during the early thirties. Not unlike Sandy Koufax three decades later, Dean utterly dominated his league for a few memorable years. Between 1932 and 1936, he was easily the best pitcher in the National League. In 1937, he suffered an injury to his toe during the All-Star Game; he tried to return to action too soon, altered his pitching style, and hurt his arm. He was never the same on the mound; although, as a member of the Cubs in 1938, he was able to fashion a strong curveball that replaced his legendary, but now absent, fastball. Dean was a key contributor to the Chicago pennant effort in that year, although he lost the Series game he started against the Yankees, and the Cubs were swept, 4 to 0.

Dean never rose to the heights as a player for a full season again. After the 1941 season, he found himself out of baseball. He built a new career as a popular radio broadcaster for the St. Louis Browns; in 1947, after lambasting the team's pitching staff for months over the airwaves, the forty-three-year-old former star stepped onto the mound and pitched in the last game of the Browns' season. Dean shut out the White Sox for four innings and went 1-for-1 at the plate!

In summary: Given the five-man rotation and the quick hook most modern managers see fit to apply to their starting pitchers, it's a good bet we've seen the last of the 30-game winners. Was Dean one of them? It makes good copy to say yes, but it ain't necessarily so. If you take away Dean's disputed win, the last true-blue 30-game winner turns out to be Lefty Grove, who won 31 pitching for the 1931 Philadelphia Athletics. Some people might argue that we shouldn't go back and fix the books when we find a mistake like the one that mars Dean's record, but ample precedent exists. (See Myth 41, which relates the story of the controversial 1910 batting race.) Grove's incredible season, and Denny McLain's extraordinary 1968 season with the Detroit Tigers stand out all the more when Dean's controversial "victory" is accounted for—and is that really such a bad thing?

MYTH 4

Only Players Get Beaned

Now the men at the plate wear fancy headgear,
But the fans in the stands, too, have reason for fear.

Big-league baseball has had its share of infamous beanball incidents: the Ray Chapman tragedy (see Myth 8), Tony Conigliaro's career-shattering injury at the plate, and Dickie Thon's similarly terrifying encounter with an all-but-lethal pitched ball. These much-discussed events remind us of the dangers every batter faces when he steps up to the plate to face a big-league pitcher. But most baseball fans don't stop to think of the possibility that *they themselves* may be taking their lives into their hands when they hand their ticket over to the man at the turnstile and take their seats in the ballpark.

The back of that ticket, by the way, features, in tiny print, language distancing big-league baseball from any liability arising from batted or thrown balls (or other equipment) striking the spectator in question. In other words, your baseball ticket is not just a ticket. It's a contract. The deal is a simple one—if you want to see a game, you do so by paying the ticket price *and* agreeing that if something white and round comes hurtling your way from the field and creams you, neither you, nor any of your surviving loved ones, can sue the ballclub or the game as a whole for negligence. Gives you a warm feeling inside, doesn't it?

But what's the big deal? It's not as if spectators face any real danger in going to a baseball game, right?

Well, that all depends on how we define "real danger." If what's under discussion is "statistically significant risk," then no, attending a baseball game almost certainly doesn't increase the odds of something awful happening to you by any appreciable amount. In fact, the drive to the park is probably more dangerous than the game itself. (And if you live in or near Boston, Massachusetts, you know that negotiating traffic around Kenmore Square, as a motorist *or* a pedestrian, is the type of activity that makes insurance actuaries cringe.)

But if we define "real danger" as "awful things that were highly unlikely but happened anyway, and may do so again at any moment for all we know," then an honest assessment of the situation yields some reason for concern. After all, baseball bigwigs wouldn't put that fine print on the back of the tickets if people *never* got smacked by hurtling leather spheres, right? And with 81 home games per year, each attracting thousands of spectators, and each featuring any number of potentially dangerous batted or thrown balls, the question isn't *whether* something terrifying is likely to happen in the stands of your local big-league park, but *when*.

The one-in-a-million shot, in other words, doesn't seem all that implausible when you're the one in a million.

Can incredibly weird stuff happen? Sure. Consider the following. On May 14, 1939, Bob Feller was pitching for the Cleveland Indians against the Chicago White Sox at Comiskey Park. In the third inning, Chicago Batter Marvin Owen took a swing at a Feller offering and sent a screaming line drive foul into the stands behind first base. The line drive struck a female spectator square in the face. She was rushed to the hospital, where she spent several days under obervation, and where Feller himself came to visit and monitor her progress.

He had a special interest in the case. The female fan who'd been struck was Feller's own mother.

By the way, she was in attendance with her family as guest of honor at the park. The game in question took place on Mother's Day!

Mrs. Feller was eventually released; she apparently recovered without complications from her injury, which, though extremely painful, was not life-threatening.

The same, alas, cannot be said for the spectator who happened to be in the stands before a Washington Senators game in the 1940s. Infielder Sherry Robinson unleashed a throw during infield practice that *hit and killed* a fan who was sitting in the seats behind first base!

In summary: Keep your eyes peeled when you go to the park...and bring along that rabbit's foot, just in case. Come to think of it, bringing along a batting helmet of your own might not be such a bad idea, either.

MYTH 3

Ty Cobb Stroked 4,191 Lifetime Base Hits

How many hits did the Georgia Peach make?
The true answer, fans, is no piece of cake.

Numbers. Sometimes it seems as though fans can't live without them.

Baseball is a number-intensive game, perhaps the *most* number-intensive of all games. A good deal of its allure can be traced to its fans' infatuation with the statistics it generates constantly. Day in, day out, week in, week out, season in, season out—during the baseball season, there is always a new set of numbers to look at, as well as an old set of numbers to which to compare the new set. We trust the morning box score, I think, in a way that we don't rely on a football game's printout of events, dotted as it is with a futile series of minute-and-second references. Somehow we *need* a baseball box score more, because we trust it to represent something that is fundamentally timeless and right and beyond minutes and seconds. Perhaps we want baseball information to help us transcend the passage of time. It's part of the game's promise to us. So we pay close attention to the numbers it gives us with each new, promising day.

Over the years, the numbers associated with certain baseball records come to carry a cachet that at times seems ready to overpower the achievement itself. Is there any other sport in which this happens more often than in baseball? How many football or basketball fans commit the statistics of their chosen team—or a great team from the past—to memory? How many pursue the numerical minutiae of their game's history with the eagerness that the average rabid baseball fan displays?

Ask any serious baseball fan to identify the comparative significance of the numbers 60 and 61, or the figures 714 and 755, or the simple numerical average .406, and it's a pretty good bet you'll hear the right answers. (Babe Ruth's 60 home runs in 1927, Roger Maris's 61 in 1961, Babe Ruth's 714 lifetime home runs [see Myth 21], Hank Aaron's 755 lifetime home runs, Ted Williams's batting mark for the memorable 1941 season.) Even if the record in question is *broken*, the magical sense of possibility that has resided for so many years within one of the worshiped figures may remain.

What if one of those numbers, invested for so many years with the aura of immortality, turns out to be wrong?

The question attaches itself to one of the most cherished lifetime totals in all of baseball: Ty Cobb's vaunted (and, thanks to the efforts of Pete Rose and his 4,256 career hits, now-eclipsed) supposed lifetime hit total of 4,191.

For decades the number served as a sort of mental shrine for baseball fans, a standard that seemed unlikely ever to be surpassed. Eventually it was. But the standard turned out to have been set ever so fractionally too high. Ty Cobb actually closed out his career with *4,189* hits. And despite the appearance of such distorted numbers as 4,191, 4,192, and 3,902—who knows where that *last* one came from!—in some seemingly up-to-date baseball references, 4,189 *is* the right number, and it is so listed in the thorough, exemplary *Sports Illustrated 1996 Sports Almanac*.

Why the confusion? The numbers were out of line for the 1910 season (see Myth 41), resulting in Cobb's being credited with two hits he did not make—and a batting championship that should have gone to someone else. Even if the books have been corrected—and some have—the number that still lingers in peoples' memories is that mystical, long-revered 4,191. It's as though adjusting one's *mental* record of one of the game's most sacred elements calls the whole system into account. For a good many students of the game, the number 4,189 seems, well, a little odd. Hard to say. Hard to read. Hard to remember. They revert to the inaccurate number by instinct. It feels better. Accepting the accurate one is a bit like hearing that you've got one more sibling than you thought you did. How is one supposed to manage that overnight?

Who else besides baseball fans would get misty-eyed over a series of digits?

What record was it, exactly, that Charlie Hustle broke? We owe ourselves an honest answer. Cobb's achievement—like Rose's—is breathtaking. Especially when it's rendered accurately.

In summary: Better-Late-Than-Never Department: The real lifetime hit total for the less-than-lovable spiritual predecessor of Albert Belle should read 4,189, not 4,191.

MYTH 2

Jackie Robinson Was the First Black Major-League Ballplayer

Robinson broke through the barriers laid,
But black men before Jackie had actually played.

The unforgettable Jackie Robinson assumed many roles during his playing years: a superb player, the personification of bravery in the face of hideous discrimination and abuse, and one of the two men (the other being Dodgers executive Branch Rickey) most responsible for helping to erase the color line in major-league baseball.

All that having been said, the great Brooklyn star and utterly deserving Hall of Famer was not the first black major-leaguer. He was the first black *twentieth-century* major-leaguer to win a roster spot without concealing his race. As this book has demonstrated at any number of points, confusing major-league baseball with twentieth-century baseball is an all-too-common error.

It's not generally known, but a number of black players found their way into the big leagues in the game's early years. The first seems to have been Moses Fleetwood Walker, a catcher who worked his way up from the college to the professional level, and by 1884 was a catcher for the Toledo Blue Stockings in the American Association.

One of baseball's most important early stars, Chicago's

Adrian "Cap" Anson (an unrepentant racist) once refused to play the Toledo team because Walker was a part of it. Anson's oft-expressed view was—quoting now—that "gentlemen do not play baseball with niggers." That game was played, but under protest. In a game against Richmond, Toledo's manager received a letter threatening a riot if Walker dared to set foot on the field. (As it happened, Walker, who had been injured, was not going to play anyway.) When a paper in the hometown of a rival club jeeringly called Walker a "coon," a spirited defense of the black catcher appeared in the *Sporting News*.

Walker finished up his only season in the big leagues with a respectable .263 average. Among the other black major-leaguers of the era were Frank Stovey (also of Toledo), Frank Grant of Buffalo, and Robert Higgins of Syracuse. All endured abuse from racist players, fans, and team officials.

Thanks in part to Anson's lobbying, racial segregation eventually became established practice among mainstream teams. "[Anson's] repugnant feeling," one observer wrote in 1907, "shown at every opportunity, toward colored players, as a source of comment throughout every league in the country, and his opposition, with his great power and popularity in baseball circles, hastened the exclusion of the black man from the white leagues." But it was not always so, even though the black players who did don uniforms for their teams always faced extraordinary challenges.

It should go without saying that the existence of a (brief) period during which some blacks played at the major-league level does not in the least diminish Robinson's achievement in 1947, when he broke in with the Dodgers. Baseball—and America—needed Jackie Robinson, whether it knew about that need or not. Robinson showed unbelievable discipline, self-control, and devotion to the game during his time with the Dodgers. He was a man on a mission, and he was also an exceptional athlete who stayed on with his team for the best of all possible reasons: He helped them win pennants. Of how many other great careers was big-league baseball deprived between the early 1890s—when the color line solidified—and 1947?

Robinson was a one-of-a-kind player to whom baseball, and all of America, owes a significant debt. The challenges he faced are better understood when we realize that the color line in baseball was not *always* a foregone conclusion (although it eventually became such); in the early days of big-league ball, racism was not even a unanimous matter of established team practice. Teams, naturally enough, wanted to win, and a good number of them wanted to do so by fielding the best available players.

Segregation was not part of the "natural order" of things in big-league baseball; it was, as racism always is, a conscious choice, and an appalling one. The choice was, at first, implemented uncertainly and inconsistently. Over time, the game's routine solidified into the grossly unfair policy of across-the-board discrimination in organized ball. (See Myth 42 for a discussion of how "formal" the organized-baseball ban on blacks came to be.) The policy, by the way, was one that more than one person tried to get around by passing players off as Cuban or Indian. (John McGraw tried this, with no success, with the players Oscar Charleston and Charlie Grant, respectively.) Foreign-born players with dark skin appear to have been easier for the big leagues to accept; some point to the Washington Senators of the middle thirties and early forties as one team that (quietly) crossed the color line by employing Spanish-speaking players who couldn't be classified as "white."

Moses Walker's career is unlikely to be mistaken for that of Jackie Robinson, but his experiences, and those of others who tried to make their way in the big leagues during baseball's early years, are certainly worth remembering.

In summary: Robinson was one of the game's giants; the role of players like Walker should be acknowledged as well. They, too, faced hatred, intolerance, and stupidity, and if their on-the-field accomplishments were not as remarkable as the Brooklyn star's, their off-the-field obstacles probably had a great deal in common. Walker's career serves as a reminder that the unpardonable example of racial prejudice at the major-league level did not have to come about in the first place. That it did come about, and that the game, and the country, ever needed someone as courageous and talented as Jackie Robinson to reverse it in the twentieth century, stands as an instance of national disgrace.

MYTH I

Babe Ruth Hit a "Called Shot" Home Run in the 1932 World Series Against the Chicago Cubs

The Babe is a hero, but that's not enough—
We want to believe he predicted his stuff!

In the fifth inning of the third game of the 1932 World Series, Babe Ruth hit a home run. This much is undisputed. However, the events surrounding this round-tripper have been relentlessly overblown, perhaps even beyond the imagination of the most partisan Yankee fan of the day. Ruth, the legend goes, possessed some superhuman ability to smash round-trippers at will—or at least he did on this occasion.

For six decades, the notion that the Sultan of Swat boldy pointed to the bleachers, and then parked a home run in the exact spot he'd indicated, has refused to die. It has been so widely disseminated that a good many writers either accept it without question or blithely dismiss the whole matter as something that will "probably never be resolved." But the issue can be resolved, or at least clarified, by examining where and how the story began. A breathless contemporary account of the supposed "called shot" ran in the *New York Times* on October 2, 1932:

Ruth came up in the fifth, and in no unmistakable motion the Babe notified the crowd that the nature of his retaliation would be a wallop right out of the park.

The "retaliation" envisioned by the Bambino was, we are told, occasioned by the jeers and catcalls of the boisterous Chicago fans. That's the way it reads in some stories, at any rate. In others, he's being razzed from the Cubs bench, and is so enraged at their verbal assaults that he determines to show them once and for all just what kind of hitter they're dealing with. In still other accounts, Cubs pitcher Charlie Root is the man against whom Ruth plots revenge. For decades, baseball fans have been told by "called shot" proponents that one, two, or all three of these versions reflect something that happened before Ruth predicted and hit his home run.

Everyone agrees that Ruth teed off on Root, launching the longest home run that had ever been hit in Wrigley Field. But was he really pointing to the stands, or was he, as graying Cubs and Cub fans of all ages have been insisting for years, merely gesturing toward Root? Without entering into a protracted debate over the likely veracity of partisan teammates, let us consider three points.

- Most national papers did not report anything other-worldly about the home run besides its staggering distance. Suspiciously, however, the above-quoted *New York Times* and the *New York World-Telegram* did appear to make the claim for a "called shot" of some kind. A certain hometown bias is not difficult to infer. The *Times* account makes no direct reference to Ruth pointing to center. Of the other article, Nicholas Acocella and Donald Dewey, in their *Encyclopedia of Major League Baseball Teams*, note that Joe Williams of the *World-Telegram* was the only writer in attendance at the game to

....

"suggest that [Ruth] had pointed to the center field bleachers" before launching his homer. Together, the hometown stories may very well have been the beginning of the "called shot" myth.

- The exact means by which the "shot" was "called" often depends on who's telling the story. Yankee pitcher Lefty Gomez said Ruth pointed to right field; most others who support the "called shot" story say it was center field. Ruth himself seems to have offered accounts of the home run that did not agree in all specifics.

- Finally—and this is the clincher—*Ruth did not claim credit for the "called shot" until well after it had become established as a national myth.* Anyone with even a cursory understanding of Ruth's reputation and habits of dealing with the press will have a hard time imagining the Big Guy maintaining a humble silence after such a momentous event. But there he was, smiling and ducking the issue, when asked by reporters about whether he had really predicted the home run he hit off Root. "Why don't you read the papers?" Ruth asked. "It's all right there in the papers." When he hit his sixtieth home run earlier that season, Ruth was more than forthcoming about his accomplishment. Here was, seemingly, an even greater moment...and, in the immediate aftermath of it, he seemed eager to let others do the talking. Why?

More points to ponder: The home run, which was Ruth's last in Series play, does not receive any special notice in the account of the game appearing in *The Baseball Encyclopedia*. That respected volume tactfully declines to identify anything out of the ordinary about Ruth's fifth-inning blast, noting only that "back-to-back home runs...by the two sluggers [Ruth and Gehrig] decided the game." And in response to the editorial question "True?" concerning the fateful homer, Ruth is quoted as follows in Bill Felber's *125 Years of Major League Baseball*: "Of course not, but it made a hell of a story."

One more time, from the man who ought to know: "Of course not, but it made a hell of a story."

When the Bambino himself bails out, and whole crowds of people still cling frantically to the oft-recited, deeply cherished moment of magic, you know you've come across one of the all-time whoppers, the type of *übermyth* that shows both a brazen disregard for the facts and an extraordinary staying power worthy of Gaylord Perry, Pete Rose, or Satchel Paige. (Come to think of it, Satch may have stretched a story now and then himself.)

Why has Ruth's nonprediction turned into one of the most cherished happenings in all of baseball history, the type of heroic deed people pay good money to see reproduced on a full-color collectible plate? Because the "called shot" made great copy. It *still* makes great copy, which is one reason it's so often relegated to the safely neutral "we-may-never-know-the-truth" category by fans, sportwriters, and even historians who desperately *want* to write and talk about about the home run, but probably know they shouldn't. ("Whether he was merely gesturing toward the Cub dugout or pointing at the pitcher or beyond him, into the stands, no one will ever know for sure" runs one typically distanced sentence—this one in the otherwise superb *Baseball: An Illustrated History* by Geoffrey Ward and Ken Burns. There are dozens more in any number of other books that play the same semantic games.) It's as though failing to admit that there *might* be something to the story not only deprives one of the chance to hold forth on one of the "great baseball moments," but somehow makes one less of a true baseball fan.

Baloney. Either it happened or it didn't. Take everything into account—including Ruth's own mysterious failure to boast about the deed at the time, so odd from a man who never missed an opportunity to boast about much of anything, and his own later admission of the hoax—and draw your own conclusion. If you conclude that it didn't happen, or that it may have looked for a moment like it happened to some New York reporters who knew a good story when they saw one, you can still be a good baseball fan.

And yet...it made such a glorious headline. It made such a remarkable story. It *sounded* like it could have been true. For a country in the midst of a Depression and in search of bigger-than-life heroes, maybe it *should* have been true. But the only real truth the much-discussed home run that Babe Ruth hit that day cast any light on was the ability of baseball fans to believe what they wanted to believe. It was the stuff that dreams are made of. And that's why people keep coming back to it.

In summary: Ruth was gesturing toward Cub pitcher Charlie Root, probably, as most reliable witnesses attest, in response to Root's second strike and as a reminder that he still had one strike left. Or perhaps the gesture was of a more insulting nature. That he made the most of the following pitch is beyond any argument. That he may have *looked* like he was pointing toward the stands is possible. That he *knew he was going to hit a home run*—which is what "calling one's shot" has to mean if it means anything at all—is a falsehood originated by the New York press and dutifully maintained over the decades by Yankee fans and sports sentimentalists.

Epilogue

This has been a challenging, rewarding book to write. It required some serious detective work and no small degree of patience, since many of the misconceptions and myths discussed here have been repeated for years, in their erroneous form, in various printed resources. Tracking down reliable and unbiased accounts has, in some cases, been an arduous task. But I think it's been worth it.

One of the most unexpected benefits of this project has been the way that it has allowed for a good, long look at the whole process of mythmaking. By working on this book, I've been able to gain new perspective on that process. Most people would agree, I think, that the need for myths and heroes is an inherently, uniquely human one; they'd probably also agree that, on balance, the instinct to pass along important stories about extraordinary happenings is normal, healthy, and generally praiseworthy. People need to have events and individuals to look up to, and good stories represent the best way to go about establishing those events and individuals for people who missed out on firsthand experience of the events.

The national game has always had its heroes, its extraordinary accomplishments, its breathless retellings of ennobling, thrilling deeds. Very often, of course, these accounts reflect actual events, circumstances, and trends; occasionally, they don't. Almost always, however, these accounts reflect our desire to find something transcendent, and usually distinctly American, in the National Pastime. The myth often reflects or illustrates some important core value—notable either for its presence or its absence—that people believe to be important. Such "lessons" usually rest just beneath the surface of the story: The persistence and good spirits in the face of "unparalleled" bad fortune and talentlessness shown by the 1962 Mets, say, or the triumph of sheer childlike audaciousness illustrated by Dizzy Dean's historic "30-win" season.

My view, after reviewing some of the most overblown misconceptions about the game of baseball, is that the core values that fans try so hard to support with fictitious events or misinterpreted data usually don't *need* the myth in the first place. Very often, when the facts do not support the myth, the *value* the myth sought to illustrate remains as a valid standard in baseball—and in life. Are good humor and a sense of perspective essential to the task of enduring the toughest of times? Yes they are, even though the New York Mets weren't the worst team in the history of big-league ball. Can a devoted and audaciously, gloriously, innocently self-absorbed approach to life and work sometimes lead to historic achievements? Yes it can, even though Dizzy Dean didn't win 30 games in 1934.

In attempting to justify Abner Doubleday's (nonexistent) claim as the inventor of the National Pastime, Albert G. Spalding wrote, "I claim that Base Ball owes its prestige as our national game to the fact that as no other form of sport it is the exponent of American courage, confidence, combativeness; American dash, discipline, determination; American energy, eagerness, enthusiasm; American pluck, persistence, performance; American spirit, sagacity, success; American vim, vigor, vitality."

Spalding's impassioned pleadings for Doubleday can't stand up under scrutiny, but his alliterative recitation of the virtues of the game were true then. I would argue that they are, in the game's best moments, still true today.

Here's to the best guiding ideas and values *behind* the myths. May they never be shown to be untrue.

Bibliography

Alexander, Charles C. *Our Game: An American Baseball History.* New York: Henry Holt, 1991.

Carroll, Bob. *Baseball Between the Lies.* New York: Perigee, 1993.

Dewey, Donald, and Nicholas Acocella. *Encyclopedia of Major League Baseball Teams.* New York: HarperCollins, 1993.

Felber, Bill. *125 Years of Professional Baseball.* Chicago: Triumph Books, 1994.

Forker, Dom. *The Ultimate Baseball Quiz Book.* New York: Signet, 1995.

James, Bill. *The Baseball Book, 1992.* New York: Villard Books, 1992.

Murphy, John. *The Bathroom Baseball Book.* Saddle River, N.J.: Red Letter Press, 1988.

Nemec, David. *Great Baseball Feats, Facts, and Firsts.* New York: Signet, 1995.

Obojski, Robert. *Baseball's Strangest Moments.* New York: Sterling Publishing, 1988.

Reichler, Joseph L., ed. *The Baseball Encyclopedia: The Complete and Official Record of Major League Baseball,* 6th edition. New York: Macmillan, 1985.

Shatzkin, Mike, ed. *The Ballplayers: Baseball's Ultimate Biographical Reference.* New York: Arbor House/William Morrow, 1990.

Shaugnessy, Dan. *The Curse of the Bambino.* New York: Penguin Books, 1991.

Thorn, John, ed. *The Armchair Book of Baseball II.* New York: Charles Scribner's Sons, 1987.

Thorn, John, and Pete Palmer, eds. *Total Baseball.* New York: Warner Books, 1990.

Weiss, Peter. *Baseball's All-Time Goats.* Holbrook, Mass.: Bob Adams, Inc., 1992.

———. *Longshots: The Most Unlikely Championship Teams in Baseball History.* Holbrook, Mass.: Bob Adams, Inc., 1992.

Ward, Geoffrey C., and Ken Burns. *Baseball: An Illustrated History.* New York: Alfred A. Knopf, 1994.

Zoss, Joel, and John Bowman. *Diamonds in the Rough: The Untold History of Baseball.* Chicago: Contemporary Books, 1996.

Index

About the Author

BRANDON TOROPOV is a baseball fan of long standing whose other books include *101 Reasons to Hate George Steinbrenner* and *Who Was Eleanor Rigby? . . . and 908 Other Questions about the Beatles*. He lives in Middleton, Massachusetts, with his wife Mary and their three children. Mr. Toropov hopes someday to see the designated-hitter rule abolished in the American League.